THE SMART & COMMON SENSE INVESTOR

LONG-TERM INVESTMENT STRATEGIES FOR WEALTH CREATION

LESSONS FROM A PRIVATE INVESTOR

CHINEDU CHIANA

Published in the United Kingdom by
Poshgeezer Productions

A CIP record of this book is available from the British Library.

First published in Great Britain in 2014

ISBN 978-0-9926545-1-1

Dedication

This book is dedicated to the memory of my late father and to my mother for the sacrifices they made to make me the person I am today. Also to my wife, Maureen and two sons, Peter and David, for their support and understanding during the long hours I spent writing this book.

About the author

Chinedu Chiana is a Consultant General and Breast Surgeon and a Fellow of the Royal College of Surgeons in the United Kingdom. He also has a Masters degree from the University of Kent. He has extensive experience and interest in business and personal finance. This book is based on experiences gained from over 30 years as a private investor. His other interests include sports, music and education. He is married with two sons and lives in Kent.

Links

www.thesmartlongterminvestor.com

https://twitter.com/theholdinvestor

www.facebook.com/smartlongterminvestor

Disclaimer

The author is not a registered investment or financial adviser. No information in this book should be taken as advice or recommendation to buy or sell any asset. References to companies are made for illustration purposes only. Any research, reference, information or opinion is obtained from sources believed to be reliable; however their reliability cannot be guaranteed. Neither the author nor the publisher can accept responsibility for any loss occasioned to any person who either acts or refrains from acting as a result of any statement in this book. The author may have holdings in investments referred to in the book and may add or dispose of them. The value of an investment can fall as well as rise, and you may not get back the full amount invested.

Contents

Introduction

I was over the Atlantic on British Airways Boeing 777 flight 193 from London Heathrow to Dallas Fort Worth on my way to the San Antonio Breast Cancer Symposium on December 10, 2008 when I finally made the supreme effort to start the draft for this book. I was prompted to write a book on investment for two reasons. With over 30 years' experience as an active private investor, I have tried out various investment strategies, experiencing not only significant successes but also my share of mistakes and failures. I have witnessed the exhilaration and exuberance of bull markets and the agony of bear market losses. I have educated myself through reading numerous investment books, biographies, magazines, articles and financial newspapers. I have studied the methods of the most successful investors. I have accumulated a wealth of experience and investment knowledge which I would have found invaluable at the start of my journey through the investment maze. This book is therefore a constellation of investment principles, born out of my personal experience and aimed primarily at the amateur investor as a simple guide to building a long-term portfolio of shares and wealth.

Secondly, and perhaps of more importance, this book has an educational function. There is considerable misconception and mistrust about investing in shares. Even amongst the well-educated, the degree of ignorance about the stock market is breath-taking. There is a widely held perception that investing in shares is akin to playing the roulette table where the odds are massively stacked against you. Share trading is usually accorded a higher status as a gambling venture than buying a lottery ticket – a pursuit undertaken very seriously and at great loss by many. There is also a false belief that you need to be fabulously wealthy to invest in the stock market. Shares are therefore given a wide berth by a large segment of the population who consequently lose out on the potential and opportunity to participate in the economic growth of their country and build up personal and family wealth. It is my earnest hope that this book will go some way in removing some of these myths and prejudices. This is all the more pertinent with the current drive by many nations for individuals to take more control of their pensions, retirement planning and long-term social care.

Naturally, people tend to link shares with news headlines. Stock market crashes often create an indelible negative impression in their memories. Conversely, human psychology leads to a headlong rush to invest in shares at the height of bull markets when the news bulletins are daily screaming new market highs and the stock market is the main topic of discussion at social gatherings. Regrettably, many people are tempted to invest in the market during these periods when valuations are stretched and shares present their highest risk, hoping to make a quick profit. Their fingers are severely burnt when they sell out at considerable loss as the inevitable correction ensues. Investing in such a manner is clearly a gamble devoid of any common sense or logic.

There is a glut of investment information in the public domain which has been immensely boosted by the easy access provided by the internet but unfortunately this has failed to adequately educate the populace. Awareness of the basics and principles of investing remains very low. It is a failure of both the professional investment community but more importantly of our education system. There has been a monumental failure to educate people on the benefits of investing early in life, of the long-term attraction of shares and to understand that despite the inevitable cyclical falls in asset prices it is possible to build up considerable wealth in stocks and shares by following a simple, smart and common sense approach to investing. There are numerous books on investing, most of them written by professionals but the available information is often complex, full of jargon and therefore unappealing. There is hardly any investment education in our school curriculum. The value of investing early to compound long-term returns is therefore not learned till later in life and often not at all. This is a huge disservice to the nation.

Over the long run, shares outperform all other asset classes and should constitute a significant part of an investment portfolio. However, share prices can be volatile and therefore carry a risk compared to fixed income investments like bonds and cash. This book will show how to follow a long-term strategy of investment in shares as part of wealth planning. The emphasis is on a simple, smart and common sense approach that is easy to understand. I am not attempting to reinvent the wheel. The wheel is already up and running. The principles on which this book is based are not new. However, the material has been written in a systematic fashion so the novice and amateur investor in particular will understand the fundamental principles of investment and approach them without fear or apprehension. For the professional investor, this book is a reminder that despite all the esoteric and opaque investment products in the market, the most consistent wealth from stocks and shares has been created from these simple principles. This book will not therefore dabble in any detail into other asset classes like bonds, gilts, preference shares, derivatives, futures and options, contracts for difference, hedge funds and private equity. It is quite simply a common sense guide to investing profitably in stocks for the long run which anyone can employ.

This book is based primarily on a "buy and hold" strategy of equity investment. During the recent volatile market conditions in the past decade, many professional investors have questioned the cult of equities and in particular the strategy of buying stocks and holding them for the long run.

A lot of private investors allow their emotions to dictate how they invest. They trade frequently, often based on rumours, tips or a news item. They compete against the large investment houses with their fast, computerised high-frequency trading strategies and come out losers. There are several investment strategies, styles, theories and adages. Profitable portfolios have been developed from many of these strategies especially by professionals with in-depth knowledge of the particular theme. For the amateur or novice private investor, the most consistent and rewarding strategy is to employ a simple, common sense and smart long-term buy and hold policy of a diversified portfolio of stocks and shares. It may appear boring but this is the method employed by many of the wealthiest investors in the world. This book will have served its purpose if the amateur or new investor – for whom it is primarily intended – understands and applies the strategy of long-term compound growth for wealth creation.

I make no apologies for quoting freely from some of the world's greatest investors, including Warren Buffet, Peter Lynch and Anthony Bolton. These are doyens of the investment world whom I greatly admire. As the saying goes, "if we study the giants, we are less apt to be pygmies" and, quoting Sir Isaac Newton, "if I have seen further, it is by standing on the shoulders of giants".

CHAPTER 1

What are shares?

Although it's easy to forget sometimes, a share of stock is not a lottery ticket. It's part-ownership of a business.

Peter Lynch

When buying shares, ask yourself, would you buy the whole company?

Rene Rivken

Shares, also called stocks or equities, confer part-ownership of a company. They are issued by companies as a means of raising funds to run their businesses. There are two types of shares – ordinary and preference shares. Ordinary shares are the more popular type and therefore the only one to be discussed in detail in this book. As an example, one of my companies, Poshgeezer, may decide to raise £100,000 to grow the company. It issues 100,000 shares at £1 each giving the company a market capitalisation of £100,000. If you purchase 1000 shares during the offer period for £1000, you in effect own 1% of the company. These ordinary shares are then traded on the stock market where they can be bought and sold. As a part-owner of the business you have a say in how the company is run by voting on important issues.

Not all companies have their shares listed on the stock market. The shares of unlisted companies are called unquoted shares.

Shareholder value

In general, there are two common ways to make money from your shares – from capital growth and from dividends. Companies can also increase shareholder value by repurchasing their own shares (share buy-back), paying off debt and reinvesting for future growth.

Capital growth

If the earnings of Poshgeezer grow year by year, the share price and therefore the value of the company would, barring other factors, mirror this growth over the long term. Using the company, Poshgeezer with 100,000 shares issued at £1 each as an example, after 10 years of growth in earnings, each share might now be valued at £5, giving a market capitalisation of £500,000. Correspondingly, the investor with a 1% stake purchased for £1000 now has shares valued at £5000 – a 400% capital growth. Company earnings determine the future cash flows and value that accrue to investors. Conversely, the share price may fall below the purchase price, resulting in capital losses.

Dividends

The second way to profit from your part-ownership of a company is through the periodic distribution of a proportion of the earnings to shareholders known as dividends. For example, if Poshgeezer makes an annual profit of £15,000 after tax, the company may decide to pay out £10,000 as a dividend to shareholders. With 100,000 shares outstanding, this is worth 10p per share. The 1% investor with 1000 shares therefore receives a dividend of £100. In the UK, basic income tax is deducted prior to payment.

For long-term investors, the potential cash flow they receive primarily from regular dividends is the major yardstick in share valuation. The shares of companies that pay a greater proportion of their profits as dividends are called "income shares". The utilities and major oil companies are good examples. UK companies usually pay dividends every six months whilst in the USA payment is commonly every quarter.

The shares of companies that reinvest a greater proportion of their profits in the business are called 'growth shares' and usually tend to be found in young, fast-growing companies found commonly in the technology sector.

Share buy-back

The value of your shares can also be enhanced when companies repurchase some of their own shares. This reduces the number of outstanding shares thereby enhancing the earnings attributable to each share (earnings per share). If, for example, Poshgeezer buys back half of its shares, there will be 50,000 shares left in circulation. If it earns the same profit as described previously and achieves a market capitalisation of £500,000 after 5 years, each share will now be worth £10 instead of £5. Also, the dividend of £10,000 will result in a payout of 20p per share and not 10p. Companies tend to buy back their own shares when they feel the share prices are trading at a significant discount to their true value.

Reinvestment of retained earnings

The earnings left after payment of dividends are known as retained earnings. These can be reinvested in profitable assets for future growth of the company.

Repayment of debt

Repayment of debt reduces the interest paid on the debt and therefore increases the cash flow available to shareholders, either as dividends or retained earnings. Shareholder value is added if the saved interest earns a higher rate of return than the equity capital derived from the debt. Less debt increases the financial strength of the company.

The market

Shares are bought and sold on the stock market. The natural forces of supply and demand result in short-term fluctuations in share prices. Share prices are also affected by such factors as economic cycles, political events, wars and natural disasters. It is therefore possible to lose money if you sell your shares when they are trading below their cost price. However, in the long term, the value of profitable companies and therefore their share prices will tend to mirror their earnings growth. By following a strategy of regular investing at low cost in the shares of profitable companies, ignoring short-term fluctuations in share prices and reinvesting your dividends you can build up a considerable portfolio of shares as part of your financial plan. Also, by having part-ownership of companies you are in some measure contributing to the economic growth and prosperity of the country.

Bonds

Bonds are issued by governments and companies to raise money. There are therefore two main types of bonds the investor should be familiar with.

Government bonds

UK government bonds are called gilts. In the USA they are known as treasuries. Gilts are usually issued with a face value of £100 at the prevailing interest rate. The holder receives a fixed cash payment, called a coupon, every six months until maturity when the final coupon is paid out and the holder receives the principal amount. For example, a 10-year bond issued when interest rates are 5% will pay out a fixed annual interest of £5 (the coupon) for every £100. At maturity in 10 years the holder receives the original principal of £100 back. The bonds are traded on the market and therefore are subject to the laws of supply and demand. Interest rates have a strong influence on gilt prices and yields. Prices in general tend to fall when interest rates rise as the lower fixed interest becomes unattractive. Using the above illustration, if interest rates rose to 7%, the 5% bond becomes unattractive at £100. The price will therefore fall nearer to £71 to give the fixed payment of £5 a yield of 7%. The converse happens when interest rates fall and gilt prices rise.

Corporate bonds

There are two types of corporate bonds issued by companies – investment grade and high yield.

Investment-grade bonds are issued by the more established blue chip companies whilst high-yield bonds are from higher-risk companies. Like gilts, they are traded on the market. Since there is a risk of an issuer defaulting, corporate bonds tend to have a higher yield than gilts to compensate the holder for this higher risk. The yield rises during economic downturns when many companies are financially distressed. As the economy improves and the risk of company default lessens, corporate bond prices rise with a corresponding fall in yields. In the UK, funds that invest in investment-grade bonds are found within the sterling corporate bond sector. Higher-yield bonds are found in separate higher-yield funds. Funds with a mixture of both types of corporate bonds are typically listed in the strategic bond sector.

CHAPTER 2

Understand the numbers

Everything should be made as simple as possible, but not simpler.

Albert Einstein

It has been said that figures rule the world.

Johann Wolfgang Goethe

The astute investor needs a basic knowledge of company accounts and numbers. This is useful in understanding how companies function and helps the investor screen and compare companies for investment. Just as it is important to understand the financial figures when you buy a business, it is equally critical that the investor is able to independently analyse company accounts as a part-owner of a business. The investor gains by developing an intimate knowledge of the business – understanding what economic activity the business is involved in, its financial strength, the dynamics of the business, how it makes money, how profitable it is and how it compares with competitors. The investor is better equipped to analyse and value companies for investment. This screening process is very invaluable to the smart investor.

UK companies usually publish half-yearly and annual reports and accounts. These can be obtained free by writing to the company secretary. Most companies now publish these on their websites from where they can be freely downloaded.

There are also free company report services that will send you any number of reports.

You do not need to be a mathematical guru or statistician to understand company accounts. The initial pages of a typical company report may be graced with glossy photographs and reports from the Chairman and Chief Executive which may make interesting reading but in many instances can be ignored and passed over. These executives may provide insight into the company's future prospects but, for the investor, the three most important sections of the annual report are the consolidated income statement (profit and loss account), the consolidated balance sheet and the cash flow statement. An investor should make the effort to understand what each of these represent for the particular company. As you learn to understand company accounts, you can scan through these in a few minutes and make a quick judgement on whether the company meets your investment criteria and therefore merits further detailed investigation. For a shareholder, the financial report is an opportunity to keep abreast of the company's performance.

I have selected the 2013 Annual report of Aveva Group PLC, an engineering software company, as an illustration.

Consolidated income statement

The Consolidated income statement also known as the profit and loss (P&L) Account shows the profit or loss the company has made in the last year of trading. The figures are shown next to the results from the previous year for comparison. The important data are:

Revenue: A measure of the sales or turnover of the business.

Cost of sales: The direct cost involved in generating the sales.

Gross profit: The revenue minus the cost of sales.

Operating profit: The gross profit minus other expenses like administration, marketing, distribution and research and development costs.

Profit before tax: Operating profit less any interest payments.

Profit after tax: The profit attributable to equity shareholders. Also known as earnings, this is the bottom line figure that is most important for the shareholder. It shows the profit (or loss) the company has made in the past year out of which the company may pay out dividends.

Earnings per share (EPS): The profit attributable to shareholders divided by the number of shares on issue. It therefore shows how much each share has earned. The EPS is given in various formats. *The basic EPS* is easier to understand and uses the weighted average number of shares during the financial year as the denominator. *The diluted EPS* is a more complex figure that takes into account other classes of shares like warrants and convertible bonds. Aveva plc had a *basic EPS* of 66.97p and a *diluted EPS* of 66.82p for 2013.

The adjusted or headline EPS is often quoted and is the EPS adjusted for one-off and exceptional items like income from a disposal. It therefore gives a better picture of the underlying company performance. The notes that follow the financial results show that Aveva plc had an *adjusted EPS* of 74.87p (basic) and 74.70p (diluted) for 2013.

Dividend: The income statement will often show the dividend per share (DPS) for the year. Aveva paid a total dividend of 24p per share for the 2012/13 year, 4.50p at the half-year stage and a final payment of 19.50p.

Key ratios from the income statement

Several important ratios can be derived from the income statement.

The pre-tax profit margin: This is the profit before tax as a proportion of the revenue or sales and expressed as a percentage

Pre-tax profit ÷ Sales x 100

The pre-tax profit is commonly used in preference to the post-tax profit because of the variable tax regimes in different countries and can be used to compare the performance of companies in the same business sector or industry. When making such a comparison, consider the companies with the highest profit margins. This reflects the more efficient companies with lower fixed costs in which a greater proportion of the revenue drops into the bottom line, leading to higher earnings and consequently higher dividends and reinvestment in the growth of the company. Such companies, by having a low cost base, are also better equipped to withstand economic downturns as their higher margins protect against a significant reduction in revenue.

Conversely, investment in the less efficient companies can sometimes be profitable. As they reduce their costs, improve their profit margins and become more efficient, this is usually reflected in their share prices. However, the smart investor should always consider companies with a tradition of efficiency and low cost. In this respect it is worth examining the trend in the profit margin over the previous 5–10 years.

Dividend cover: This is a measure of how many times the profits attributable to shareholders could pay out the dividend. For example, Aveva had an *adjusted diluted EPS* of 74.70p and a dividend of 24p. The earnings can pay the dividend three times and therefore the dividend cover is 3. Putting it simply, the dividend cover is calculated from

EPS ÷ DPS

The higher the dividend cover, the better the ability of the company to continue paying dividends even if profits fall. Companies with stable and predictable earnings may have a low dividend cover. These are usually large companies where a minimum dividend cover of 1.5 is acceptable. In general, especially in relation to small companies, the smart investor should look for a dividend cover of at least 2.

Growth in reinvested dividends forms a major part of the long-term returns of the smart investor. During economic downturns, several companies either cut or suspend dividend payments to conserve cash. It is therefore worthwhile to seek companies with high dividend covers that are likely to maintain payments through different economic cycles.

The price/earnings (PE) ratio: The ratio of the share price to the Earnings per share (EPS)

Share price ÷ EPS

The P/E ratio is a measure of the relationship between the share price and earnings of a company and is the most commonly used metric to value companies. It reflects how the market prices the company in relation to its earnings.

Small fast-growing companies tend to have high P/E ratios while big mature ones have low ratios. As the rate of growth of fast growers declines so does the P/E ratio. P/E ratios are also generally high during periods of market optimism when the P/E ratio of the market as a whole soars and tend to decline when optimism is very low.

Historical average P/E ratio

For an individual company where the fundamentals have not changed dramatically, it is useful to look at the historical trend in its P/E ratio which can be worked out from the 10-year record table. It is best to buy their shares when they are selling at a discount to their long-term average P/E ratio. Avoid companies trading on excessively high P/E ratios in relation to their historical mean. When they falter and earnings fail to live up to the high expectations there is usually a precipitous fall in their share prices. Conversely, it is important to understand why a company has a low P/E compared to historical levels. This may reflect poor fundamentals and deteriorating earnings.

The price/earnings to growth ratio (PEG)

The P/E ratio of companies tends to mirror their earnings growth. Where the two are balanced the P/E to growth ratio is 1. Bargains are found in stocks where the P/E ratio is less than the growth rate. A PEG (P/E to growth ratio) of 0.5 (P/E ratio is half the growth rate) is very favourable. Avoid stocks with a PEG of 2 or more.

The dividend yield: Known simply as the yield, this is the total dividend per share for the year divided by the share price as a percentage.

DPS ÷ Share Price x 100

It is therefore a measure of the dividend return expected by investors by holding the shares at that price. Young fast-growing companies tend to reinvest most of their earnings and therefore pay out a smaller proportion as dividends. They also tend to command high share prices and therefore have low dividend yields. Mature companies conversely pay a larger proportion of earnings as dividends and have high yields. Be cautious when companies show a very high dividend yield. This sometimes reflects a company in some difficulty where the share price has fallen significantly and the historic yield based on the last payment is correspondingly high. In such a situation the company may often cut or suspend future payments.

Consolidated income statement
For the year ended 31 March 2013

	2013	2012
	£000	£000
Revenue	**220,230**	195,935
Cost of sales	**(16,141)**	(16,066)
Gross profit	**204,089**	179,869
Operating expenses		
Research and development costs	**(35,539)**	(32,121)
Selling and distribution expenses	**(87,588)**	(75,008)
Administrative expenses	**(18,570)**	(15,241)
Total operating expenses	**(141,697)**	(123,370)
Profit from operations	**62,392**	56,499
Finance revenue	**4,211**	3,962
Finance expense	**(2,956)**	(2,724)
Analysis of profit before tax		
Adjusted profit before tax	**70,714**	62,276
Amortisation of intangibles (excluding other software)	**(3,946)**	(3,368)
Share-based payments	**(1,226)**	(666)
(Loss)/gain on fair value of forward foreign exchange contracts	**(796)**	308
Exceptional items	**(1,099)**	(813)
Profit before tax	**63,647**	57,737
Income tax expense	**(18,134)**	(17,769)
Profit for the year attributable to equity	**45,513**	39,968

holders of the parent

Earnings per share (pence)		
basic	**66.97p**	58.86p
diluted	**66.82p**	58.73p

Consolidated balance sheet

This is perhaps the most important statement in the company accounts. It gives a snapshot of the financial structure and strength of a company and is therefore probably the first document to read when screening companies for investment. It shows the assets and liabilities of the company and therefore its net worth. The different sections of the Balance Sheet are:

Non-current assets: The fixed company assets including property, plant, equipment, intangible assets and goodwill. Intangible assets include intellectual property like patents, copyrights and trademarks that have no physical form while goodwill is a measure of the excess amount paid over the value of assets when a company is taken over.

Current assets: Assets expected to be used within a year to run the company and therefore include inventories or stock, the company's debtors (receivables) and cash. Cash is king and so an increasing cash position from the previous year is a favourable sign.

Current liabilities: Short–term liabilities that are settled within a year and comprise trade creditors, tax and short-term borrowings including overdrafts.

Non-current or long-term liabilities: Liabilities due for payment after one year, of which the most important is the long-term borrowings of the company.

Net assets: A measure of the total assets of the company less the total liabilities.

Total equity: Usually equivalent to shareholder equity or funds, this is a measure of the interest of shareholders in the company, calculated from the sum of all the assets less the total liabilities. It is therefore often the same as the net assets of the business.

Key ratios from the balance sheet

Several important financial ratios can be derived from the consolidated balance sheet.

The current assets ratio: a measure of a company's ability to pay its short-term liabilities with its current assets

Current assets ÷ Current liabilities

A ratio of more than 2 is desirable. Especially for small companies it is very encouraging if cash and cash equivalents cover the short-term debt.

The debt/equity ratio: This is useful in judging the financial strength of a company. If cash and cash equivalents cover short-term debt, the ratio is calculated using the long-term debt as a proportion of shareholders' or total equity. When the level of both short- and long-term debt is high, the total debt is used as the numerator.

The debt/equity ratio is a measure of the indebtedness of a company and therefore of its ability to survive an economic downturn. Companies with stable operating profits and cash flow can take on significant debt but in general a high debt level in relation to total equity denotes a weak balance sheet and may reflect a risky investment. The further below 100% the debt/equity ratio is, the more attractive the business. A company that has no long-term debt or more cash than long-term debt is particularly strong and generally appealing as an investment.

Gearing: Most financial publications and websites use gearing, otherwise known as leverage, to assess the level of debt in a business, so the investor should understand how it is derived. The commonest definition is the ratio of debt to capital employed to run the business calculated as a percentage:

Debt ÷ Capital employed x 100

Capital employed = debt + shareholders' equity

In general the smart investor should avoid companies with a gearing of over 50%.

Returns on shareholders' equity (ROE): this is calculated as

Earnings (post-tax profit) ÷ Shareholders' equity

This is a quick way to measure the returns shareholders are earning on their funds and is therefore a reflection of how efficiently capital is deployed. It is more useful in assessing companies in the same industry. Companies with high levels of debt will have correspondingly low shareholder equity and therefore a high ROE which may be deceptive. Never use an individual valuation parameter in making a decision on investment. Always look at the complete picture and in particular try to understand the various values as they apply to the particular company.

Return on capital employed (ROCE): a measure of the return a company is making from the total capital employed in the business, which is a combination of shareholders' funds and debt. The earnings before interest and tax (EBIT) is used. EBIT is usually similar to the operating profit.

EBIT ÷ Capital employed (Shareholders' funds + Debt)

By using the company debt in the calculation, ROCE is usually lower than ROE. ROCE measures the efficiency of capital deployment. Investors should look for companies with a high ROCE relative to their peers.

Consolidated balance sheet
31 March 2013

	2013	2012
	£000	£000
Non-current assets		
Goodwill	40,527	30,839
Other intangible assets	25,041	18,605
Property, plant and equipment	9,150	8,042
Deferred tax assets	6,291	4,009
Other receivables	1,113	811
	82,122	62,306
Current assets		
Trade and other receivables	80,277	68,054
Financial assets	-	223
Treasury deposits	136,085	130,282
Cash and cash equivalents	54,272	48,669
Current tax assets	1,865	589
	272,499	247,817
Total assets	354,621	310,123
Equity		
Issued share capital	2,269	2,266
Share premium	27,288	27,288
Other reserves	17,712	14,971
Retained earnings	204,337	176,937
Total equity	251,606	221,462
Current liabilities		
Trade and other payables	73,543	67,995

Financial liabilities	**574**	-
Current tax liabilities	**9,858**	8,936
	83,975	76,931
Non-current liabilities		
Deferred tax liabilities	**2,081**	1,855
Retirement benefit obligations	**16,959**	9,875
	19,040	11,730
Total equity and liabilities	**354,621**	310,123

Consolidated cash flow statement

The cash flow statement shows the movement of cash in and out of the company during the financial year. It shows the net cash flows from operating, investing and financing activities. The operating cash flow is particularly important. It is always reassuring to see annual increments in the amount of cash generated from the business. Companies that generate excess cash are able to pay out increasing dividends from year to year, often declare special one-off dividends and can deploy resources to grow the business through acquisitions.

Consolidated cash flow statement
For the year ended 31 March 2013

	2013	2012
	£000	£000
Cash flows from operating activities		
Profit for the year	45,513	39,968
Income tax	18,134	17,769
Net finance revenue	(1,255)	(1,2386)
Amortisation of intangible assets	4,022	3,451
Depreciation of property, plant and equipment	2,599	2,161
Loss on disposal of property, plant and equipment	254	35
Share-based payments	1,226	666
Difference between pension contributions paid and amounts charged to operating profit	(261)	(413)
Changes in working capital		
Trade and other receivables	(11,136)	5462
Trade and other payables	429	(2,848)
Changes to fair value of forward foreign exchange contracts	796	(308)
Cash generated from operating activities before tax	60,321	64,705
Income taxes paid	(19,567)	(16,927)
Net cash generated from operating activities	40,754	47,778
Cash flows from investing activities		
Purchase of property, plant and equipment	(3,862)	(2,601)

Purchase of intangible assets	**(1,341)**	(583)
Acquisition of subsidiaries and business undertakings, net of cash acquired	**(12,485)**	(5,749)
Proceeds from disposal of property, plant and equipment	**693**	110
Interest received	**1,736**	1,471
Purchase of treasury deposits (net)	**(5803)**	(7,280)
Net cash used in investing activities	**(21,062)**	(14,632)
Cash flows from financing activities		
Interest paid	**(165)**	(22)
Purchase of own shares	**(615)**	(563)
Proceeds from the issue of shares	**3**	-
Dividends paid to equity holders of the parent	**(14,602)**	**(12,832)**
Net cash flows used in financing activities	**(15,379)**	**(13,417)**
Net increase in cash and cash equivalents	**4,313**	**19,729**
Net foreign exchange difference	**1,290**	(1,245)
Opening cash and cash equivalents	**48,669**	30,185
Closing cash and cash equivalents	**54,272**	48,669

CHAPTER 3

The argument for shares

Stocks have always outperformed other financial assets for the patient investor.

Jeremy Siegel

The investor has a choice of several asset classes for investment. In addition to stocks they include property, bonds, commodities and cash. There are various proposals and recommendations on the allocation of capital to each asset class when building an investment portfolio. In particular there is debate about the relative merits of shares and fixed income assets like bonds and cash and about which asset makes the best long-term investment. Professor Jeremy Siegel, in his book, *Stocks for the Long Run*, presented extensive data and research to show that, in the long run, through market peaks and troughs, stocks were the best and safest route to wealth accumulation, surpassing other financial assets. They provide the best hedge against inflation – the biggest enemy of investment returns.

Shares versus bonds and cash

Over the long haul equities have beaten inflation and the returns from cash and bonds. Barclays Capital has published the Equity Gilts Study annually since 1956 which compares the short- and long-term returns from equities, cash deposits and bonds. The glaring picture that emerges shows that the longer the investment period, the greater the probability that the returns from shares will outperform those from bonds and cash. Over a period of two consecutive years, shares beat deposits 67% of the time and bonds 69% of the time. Over 5, 10 and 20 years shares beat both cash and bonds over 75%, 90% and 98% of the time respectively. Over 30 years it is virtually 100% of the time. As an illustration, £100 invested at the end of 1899 to the end of 2010 with gross income reinvested would have grown to about £20,126 in a savings account, £25,916 in bonds and £1.7m in shares. However, the effect of inflation would have resulted in a real return of £286, £369 and £24,133 respectively. When equities are held for as long as 20 years, the minimum return is greater than for either gilts or cash.

Gilts show periods of outperformance. For example during the decade 2000–2010 gilts showed a real return of 2.4% compared to 0.6% for equities and 1.1% for cash. Over 20 years from the start of 1980 the real return from gilts was 6.3%, which beat the long-term equity real return of 5.3%. Over the same period, USA bonds returned 6.0%, almost matching the 6.3% long-term return of equities.

The Credit Suisse Global Investment Returns Yearbook 2013 reports that over the last 113 years, from 1900 to 2013, the real value of UK equities, with income reinvested, grew by a factor of 316.0 as compared to 5.5 for bonds and 2.9 for bills. Since 1900, equities beat bonds by 3.9% and bills by 4.3% per year. The long-term annual real return from UK equities was 5.2% while bonds and cash returned 1.5% and 0.9% respectively.

Over the same period, USA equities with income reinvested grew by a factor of 951.7 compared to 9.4% for bonds and 2.7% for bills. Equities beat bonds by 4.4% and bills by 5.3% per year. Equities had an annual real return of 6.3%, bonds 2.0% and bills 0.9%. The global annual real returns are 5.0% for equities compared to 1.8% and 0.9% for bonds and US bills.

Inflation over the decade 1900–2000 has averaged about 4.1% in the UK, according to a study by the investment bank ABN Amro and the London Business School, with £1 in 1900 having the same purchasing power as £54 in 2000. Equities have been the best-performing asset class against inflation over the long term.

Shares versus property

According to figures released by Halifax, the average house price in 1959 was £2507. This is equivalent to about £43,000 in 2009 when the average price was £162,085. This is a rise of 273% after inflation or an average annual real return of 2.7%. Figures from Barclays Capital show that over the same period, shares by contrast returned 1180% after inflation or an average annual real return of 5.2% with dividends reinvested.

Over periods of more than 10 years to 2009, shares greatly outperformed property. The annual returns over 40 years are 4.4% for shares and 3% for property. Over 30 and 20 years shares returned 7.1% and 4.6% a year respectively whilst the equivalent returns from property were 2.5% and 1.5%. During the decade between 1999 and 2009, property prices surged, returning a whopping 62% or an average of 5% annually whilst shares lost about 1.2% annually with reinvested dividends (or 4.4% without).

Commodities

Over the long term the returns from investing in commodities have compared favourably with long-term equity returns. However, historically they tend to go through long periods of poor performance followed by periods of good returns like the recent resurgence in the price of gold and oil.

Equities, property and commodities all make excellent long-term investments and each have their place in a diversified portfolio. However equities, by their superior performance in the long run should constitute the largest proportion of a long-term portfolio.

CHAPTER 4

Before you invest

Investing without research is like playing stud poker and never looking at the cards.

Peter Lynch

The investor's chief problem and even his worst enemy is likely to be himself.

Benjamin Graham

Long-term investment in shares can be financially rewarding. The smart investor should consider several issues before investing in shares.

Define your financial goals and objectives

You have to define your financial goals. The quote from Ralph Seger is instructive: "an investor without investment objectives is like a traveler without a destination". The case for shares as a long-term investment to preserve purchasing power is clear. However, in the short-term shares can be risky investments with volatility in share prices and you may lose a substantial portion of your investment. If you have a short-term investment horizon of less than 5 years, for example planning for school fees, retirement or to purchase a car, your safest bet is to leave your money in a cash savings account. In the same vein, an investor close to retirement may be advised to sell part of an investment portfolio to preserve some of the accumulated wealth and avoid the significant capital losses that occur in bear markets. On the contrary, where there is a long-term investment objective, equities should constitute the predominant asset class.

Establish cash reserves

It is prudent to have some cash reserves to cover emergencies. A level equivalent to about 3–6 months' salary is advisable to cover the critical period before any insurance payments kick in.

Buy a house

A house is probably the most prudent investment most people will make. You should therefore consider purchasing a house before investing in the stock market. The attraction of buying a house derives from the leverage a mortgage provides. For example, if the price of a property on which you put down a 15% deposit increases in value by 5%, the return on your investment is 33%. Also, houses are bought as a long-term investment. Unlike the behaviour of many investors, you don't buy and sell your house based on the latest hot tip or market report on house prices. It is also unusual to sell your home because the value has risen hoping to buy it back when prices fall. We buy our houses in the knowledge that over the long term, due to the forces of supply and demand in housing, house prices will rise to provide a profitable investment. Unfortunately we do not invest in shares in the same manner.

Pay off your debts – know your personal balance sheet and net worth

Similar to a company consolidated balance sheet, it is useful for the smart private investor to evaluate their financial strength by constructing a personal or family balance sheet. List all your assets like cash, cars, real estate, furniture, computers, cameras and clothes. Try to give a reasonable value to all your assets. Subtract the value of all your liabilities including the mortgage, loans, bank overdraft, credit and store card debt, bills and other liabilities. This gives your net financial or economic worth. If you have considerable debt with a negative net worth, financial prudence dictates you should pay off your debt before investing in the stock market. All else being equal, as your debt and liabilities decrease there is a corresponding improvement in your economic and financial strength.

Do your homework and research

In the same manner you will not go out and buy a car or a television without doing some research, the smart investor must do their homework before investing in shares. Quoting Jason Zweig, an American columnist, "If we bought stocks the same way we buy socks, we would all be a lot better off". Success in any sphere of human activity comes with hard work. Sports superstars like Lionel Messi, Tiger Woods, Roger Federer and Lewis Hamilton have made their mark through years of devotion, practice and graft. Similar commitment is required to be a successful investor. Be prepared to devote time to your investments. Learn how stock markets work, the dynamics of companies in different industries and how to screen the large universe of shares to pick out those worth your money. Understand what a specific company does and how to analyse the income statement, balance sheet and cash flow statement in company accounts. By doing some research and analysing some of the valuation yardsticks already described in this book, you increase the odds of investing in your favour. This is also relevant when investing through a collective fund like a unit trust or investment trust where knowledge of the constituents, cost, management and long-term outlook and performance is worthwhile.

Ignore the experts

If you select your investments after diligent and rigorous research and understand the fundamentals that drive the companies in which you are a part-owner you should learn to ignore the so-called experts. Investing and following the progress of a select group of companies gives you an amateur's advantage. You should learn to ignore the ever-changing and contrasting brokers' pronouncements. It is common to find a company recommended as a buy on the same day another broker is recommending a sell. A company may be recommended as a buy one month, a hold the next and a sell the following month. These are usually based on short-term considerations and may affect the company's share price accordingly. Unless there is significant change in the company fundamentals, the smart investor who is equipped with an intimate knowledge of the long-term attractions should ignore any negative recommendations. Any consequent share price fall may present a buying opportunity.

Know your temperament and psychology

Of all the factors that determine your returns from the stock market, this is perhaps the most important. You need diligence and consistency to do the necessary homework and research essential for investing in financially strong industries with excellent long-term prospects. Unlike other investments or purchases we make, there seems to be a reverse psychology when it comes to investing in shares. There is a tendency to invest at the time of greatest optimism in the stock market. During the periodic peaks in share prices, when the market is overvalued and the news headlines are daily belting out another rise in share prices there is a mass and blind stampede into shares hoping to make a quick profit. Professional managers use these periods of frenzy to mop up some of the demand by launching new funds. There is speculative and greedy buying of shares not based on fundamentals. As soon as the inevitable correction arrives there is profound panic with these ill-prepared short-term investors selling out and often incurring heavy losses. This is gambling or speculation and not common sense or smart investing.

Buying high and selling low is unlike any other human commercial activity. Quoting James Grant, "In almost every walk of life, people buy more at lower prices; in the stock market they seem to buy more at higher prices". We seek bargains and discounts when we shop. You are likely to buy a few more bottles if you find the price of your favourite champagne reduced by 50%. During periods of grave pessimism, when great companies with sound fundamentals are selling at bargain prices and low valuations, we are panicked into cash and bonds which are inferior long-term investments and fear to invest in shares. If you have done your homework well and bought profitable companies, with consistent earnings and favourable long-term prospects at a reasonable price, you should use such periods of decline as a rare long-term buying opportunity to add to your portfolio or to invest in companies for the first time that previously were overvalued. Quoting Jeremy Siegel, "fear has a far greater grasp on human action than does the impressive weight of historical evidence". Or, as Warren Buffet would say, "occasional outbreaks of those two super-contagious diseases, fear and greed, will forever occur in the investment community. The timing of these epidemics is equally unpredictable, both as to duration and degree. Therefore we never try to anticipate the arrival or departure of either. We simply attempt to be fearful when others are greedy and to be greedy only when others are fearful." The smart investor should understand the short-term volatility of share prices but instead focus on the long-term growth and profitability of the business. Quoting Benjamin Graham, "in the short run, the market is a voting machine but in the long run it is a weighing machine".

Investor psychology cycle

Investors tend to behave according to the investor psychology cycle shown below. They are contemptuous when the market is at its low point. There is doubt and suspicion and investors seek the safety of cash deposits and bonds. As the market gradually recovers most investors remain wary and cautious. The smart investor has continued investing for the long run. As the markets continue to rise, more confidence returns and most investors start buying shares, having perhaps missed most of the rise. The period of great enthusiasm usually signifies the top of the bull market when there is much greed and conviction. Everyone has a "hot tip" and the stock market is the topic of discussion at every social gathering. Numerous new funds are launched, there are record company mergers and acquisitions and new companies use the opportunity to list on the market through initial public offers (IPOs). The smart investor is cautious and perhaps uses the opportunity to take some profits. There is indifference to the obvious over-valuation, a lack of interest and dismissal as the market starts to fall. This leads to denial that it would fall any further but as the slump continues panic, fear and contempt ensue. Shares are sold in the mêlée that follows, losses are incurred and many vow never to buy shares ever again. A lot of investment fingers are burnt but few lessons are learned as the next bull market returns.

The Investor Psychology Cycle

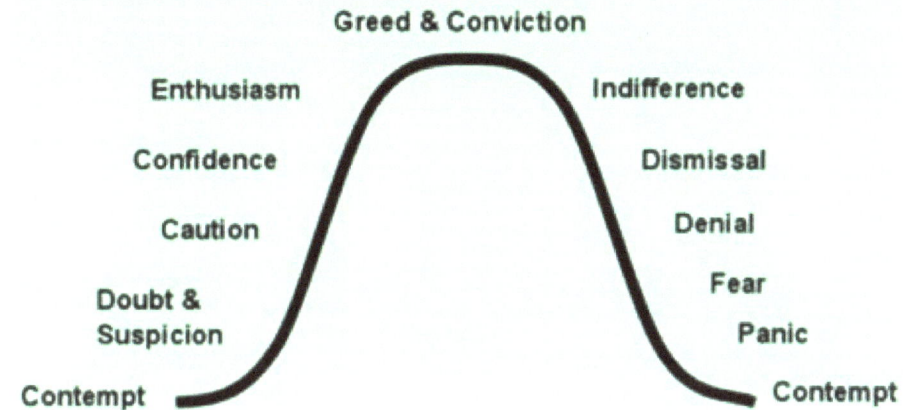

Greed & Conviction

Enthusiasm   Indifference

Confidence   Dismissal

Caution   Denial

Doubt & Suspicion   Fear

       Panic

Contempt   Contempt

Courtesy RMB Unit Trusts

Avoid excessive trading

Hyperactivity is the enemy of investment returns. Excessive trading, rushing in and out of shares, incurring high dealing charges, chasing the latest hot tip and being swayed by short-term market fluctuations will not produce a consistent return. When it comes to investing in shares, being boring is a wonderful asset. You need to develop an independent detachment from the daily market sentiment and gyrations. As long as the fundamental story remains positive, patience and masterly inactivity often reward the long-term investor.

The principles of successful investing are not dissimilar to those in other fields of human endeavour. The common sense and smart investor should be disciplined and avoid selling in a panic, confident to stay the course, but be flexible and change course when necessary, be self-reliant and detached from market sentiment, have the humility and courage to admit to mistakes and learn from them, have the ability to undertake independent research and be persistent in sticking to their strategy.

CHAPTER 5

The long-term investment strategy

Stocks are the asset of choice for virtually all investors seeking long-term growth.

Jeremy Siegel

Our favourite holding period is forever.

Warren Buffet

The evidence for the outperformance of shares over other asset classes over the long term is well established. They offer a hedge against the ravages of inflation. The smart investor should develop a long-term strategy of share investment to maximise the potential returns from a share portfolio.

Buy and hold

A "buy and hold" strategy in which shares are purchased and held long-term is the most consistent investment approach to build long-term wealth. Active trading strategies, seeking to take advantage of short-term volatility in share prices have been advocated as superior to the "buy and hold" approach. Such short-term trading, of which day trading is the most extreme, is rarely rewarding after taking into account trading costs and taxes accumulated from the high turnover. Shares should form a significant part of the portfolio of the long-term smart investor who should concentrate on buying excellent companies at reasonable valuations and holding them for the long term. The core "buy and hold" strategy of the long-term investor has recently been subjected to adverse commentaries because of the recent bear market in share prices and the relative outperformance of bonds in the last decade. Some writers have gone as far as proclaiming the demise of the strategy. The smart common sense investor should draw solace from the fact that the smartest and wealthiest investor, Warren Buffet, is the champion advocate of the "buy and hold" strategy. No argument is more compelling.

There will be periods when shares experience significant losses as occurred recently in 2008–2009. The smart investor should not be panicked into selling but should instead view these as unique buying opportunities to add to a long-term portfolio of excellent companies and thereby lower their average purchasing price. By March 2009, shares had fallen by about 50% from their previous high. Jeremy Siegel has shown that following such falls, the real return from shares over the next 30 years averages in excess of 10% per year. The Barclays Capital Equity Gilt study asserted that the equity valuations in the UK at the beginning of 2009 were at their most attractive levels for over 25 years. For the disciplined smart long-term investor, that period may prove to be one of the most profitable in history in which to buy equities. The stock market subsequently staged a powerful recovery from the end of March 2009.

The magic of compound interest

The compounding of long-term returns from shares is probably the strongest argument for a "buy and hold" strategy. Compound interest is the best friend of the long-term investor. According to Albert Einstein, it is the greatest invention of all time. It is without doubt the most critical mathematical equation the smart investor should have etched indelibly in their mind. It is a comforting beacon during periods of market volatility and depression when the natural tendency is for despondency, agitation and worry.

The power and magic of compounding returns should provide a calming solace.

Why is compound interest so valuable? Take time to understand how it works and the implications. Invested money earns an interest on the capital. The following year, interest is earned on the principal plus interest from the first year. During the third year interest is earned on the principal and the interest from the previous two years. This is illustrated in the formula:

$$M = P (1 + i)^n$$

M = final amount including principal
P = principal amount
i = rate of interest per year
n = number of years invested

The formula clearly illustrates the importance of investing for the long term. The benefits of compounding can be strongly harnessed by starting investments early in life, especially for investment horizons beyond 20 years.

Invest early

Financial investments should form part of our school curriculum to educate children on the powerful wealth that can accrue from investing from a young age. There have been tentative attempts to introduce the cult of early investment for children in the UK. Every child born in the UK from September 1, 2002 was given a £250 voucher by the government to be invested in a child trust fund (CTF). Children from low-income families received an additional £250. A further £250 (£500 for low-income families) was added at 7 years. A total of £1200 could be paid into the account annually by parents, family and friends. The government contribution was cut to £50 for children born after August 2010. All returns are tax free and the children can only withdraw funds when they turn 18. It is possible to accrue a considerable investment through this programme. For example the Children's Mutual calculates that a top-up contribution of £100 a month (which equates to the maximum allowance of £1200 a year) from birth would lead to £36,088 fund at the age of 18, assuming an investment return of 7%, charges of 1.5% and including the £250 top-up at 7 years. The CTF scheme represented a wonderful opportunity to teach children and equally their parents the value of long-term equity investment and in particular the power of compounding returns.

The CTF is now closed to new investors and was replaced in November 2011 by the Junior Individual Saving Account (JISA) which has no government contributions but allows parents, grandparents, friends and relatives to save up to £3720 (for 2013/14) annually tax free in cash or stocks and shares. The child can take over the investment at 16 but cannot touch the money till 18 when the saving turns into a standard Individual Savings Account (ISA). This is a great way to build up capital for a child. As a long-term savings plan, an equity investment has the potential to produce considerably better returns than a cash account. With an investment horizon of over 20 years and employing the magic of compound interest and dividend reinvestment it should be possible to build up sizeable investment portfolios by investing from an early age. Sadly this message is not conveyed strongly enough to our children and their parents.

Investment growth rate

The second equally important deduction to make from the equation is the significant leverage effect on returns from even a 1% difference in the rate of interest or growth. For example, £1000 invested at a compounded rate of 7% will be worth £1967 after 10 years and £2159 at 8% – a difference of £192. Over 20 years the corresponding figures are £3870 and £4661 – a difference of £791. This is particularly relevant when comparing collective funds where high costs and expense ratios can significantly diminish the long-term total return.

Reinvestment of dividends

The ability of shares to outperform other asset classes over the long term is enhanced by the reinvestment of dividends. Reinvested dividends buy more shares in the company and this process is compounded over time through the magic of compound interest. For example, if an investor with 1000 shares in a company receives an annual dividend of £10 when they cost £1 per share and reinvests the full sum, he will now own an additional 10 shares if dealing costs are excluded. The following year, dividend will be earned on 1010 shares and this is reinvested in further shares. This process compounds over time with the regular reinvestment of dividends. For the long-term investor, a dividend reinvestment strategy is indispensable and represents a very vital component of a "buy and hold" investment approach. Companies with a long history of unbroken growth in dividends, often running over more than 20 years, should be an invaluable part of a share portfolio of the smart investor. Several companies maintain Dividend Reinvestment Plans (DRIPs) that allow investors to reinvest their cash dividends in more shares of the company at low cost. Similarly, most online broking accounts allow for automatic dividend reinvestment which the smart long-term investor should always sign up to.

The Credit Suisse Global Investment Returns Yearbook 2009 study shows that an initial sum of $1 invested in US equities in 1900 grew, with dividends reinvested, at an annualised rate of 9.2% per year to become $14,276 by the end of 2008, growing in purchasing power by 582 times when inflation is taken into account. This corresponds to an annualised real return of 6.0%. Without dividend reinvestment, the initial $1 would have grown to just 6 times its initial value over the 109 years, equivalent to a real capital gain of 1.7% per year – an almost 100 times difference in value creation. For UK equities, the 2013 Barclays Equity Gilt Study shows that £100 invested at the end of 1899 would in real terms be worth £160 by the end of 2012. With reinvestment of dividends this would have grown to an outstanding £22,239.The annualised real return of UK shares is about 5.3%. There is no better illustration of the power of compound interest and dividend reinvestment.

Long-term share returns

Elroy Dimson, Paul Marsh and Mike Staunton at the London Business School produce the market analysis for the Credit Suisse study. They show that the long-term returns from shares derive from three sources – dividends, growth in dividends and share price performance as reflected in the price/earnings (P/E) ratio.

In the short term, share prices are volatile and therefore most returns are from capital gains or losses whilst dividends play a minor role. Over a one-year period share price performance accounts for over 80% of value, diminishing to less than 50% after 10 years. Conversely, long-term returns are dominated by the compounding value of reinvested dividends which increase in prominence the longer the investment horizon. Up to 90% of the long-term equity returns derive from dividend growth and reinvestment. The significance of reinvested dividends to the equity returns of the smart long-term investor cannot be over-emphasised.

Growth in earnings

Companies add value through capital appreciation or growth in the share price. The long-term investor should look for companies with a consistent growth in sales and earnings over a long period. Over the long term the share prices of such companies will grow to reflect the growth in earnings. A short-term spurt in earnings can occur because of a new product or service which may not be sustainable. A company with a long history of consistent growth in earnings per share is more likely to continue such growth in the future. Companies with a long history usually publish their 10-year record towards the back of the annual report. Companies with at least a 10% or more compounded annual growth are particularly attractive.

Market capitalisation

Companies grow their earnings at different rates. Companies listed on the stock market are grouped into small, medium and large sizes depending on their market capitalisations. The market capitalisation of a company is derived from the number of shares on issue multiplied by the share price. The fastest growth in earnings is usually found in small companies where a compounded annual rate of 20–25% can often be found in some young enterprises. This is not usually sustainable over a long period and so the investor should aim for at least a 12% growth rate from small companies. Amongst these will be companies where the share price will double in 5 years. These fast growers usually reinvest a greater proportion of their earnings in growing the business and therefore have low dividend yields.

What is considered a small company varies between markets. In the UK this includes companies with a market capitalisation of less than £200m. Many of them are listed on the FTSE Alternative Investment Market (Aim). Their share prices tend to fall faster in a market downturn. In 2008 when the Aim All-Share Index fell more than 62%, the FTSE Small Cap index fell by about 46% whilst the FTSE 100 index of large companies was down by 31%. The share prices of fast-growing small companies may also experience large falls when their growth rate falters. Over the long haul, UK smaller companies have outperformed larger ones by an annualised average of about 2.3%.

Large companies have a slow, almost predictable growth in earnings of about 5–7%. They pay a higher proportion of earnings as regular dividends and consequently have high dividend yields. Amongst these are some blue chip companies with a long history of consistent growth in sales and earnings, strong financial strength and sound long-term fundamentals. A share portfolio for the long term should have a mixture of companies with different market capitalisations.

CHAPTER 6

The perfect company

You should invest in a business that even a fool can run, because someday a fool will.

Warren Buffet

Every stock you own should have an investment thesis.
Anthony Bolton

The new investor often faces the often daunting challenge of deciding which companies to invest in and at what price. There are proponents of different investment methods and styles. Value investors look for shares selling at low valuations that usually pay a significant part of their earnings as dividends, while growth investors seek out fast-growing companies with low dividend yields. Companies can be purchased based on their market capitalisation – small, medium-sized and large companies. Some investors look for cyclical companies whose revenues and earnings fluctuate with the economic cycle like the airlines and motor industry. The strategy is to buy them at the low point of the cycle and reap the profits when the economy is booming again. Other investors look for turnaround companies that are experiencing severe difficulties with poor prospects where a restructuring sometimes leads to a rebound in earnings and the share price. A contrarian approach is employed by many famous investors including Warren Buffet. They buy when everyone is selling and they can spot a bargain, and vice versa.

Purchase a business

The long-term investor should look at shares as conferring part-ownership of a business. The same diligence and thought you would apply when buying a business are equally critical when purchasing shares. You should therefore look for a business you want to own for a long period. Search for the same values you will look for in a business. You want to buy a business you understand, that has been consistently growing revenues and earnings, is profitable and financially strong, with excellent long-term prospects and selling at a reasonable valuation. When you own such a business you will not be concerned about the daily gyrations in the share price and market value or be panicked into jettisoning your shares when markets fall. Your actions will be guided solely by the performance of the business. As long as the prospects remain sound and intact you stay invested for the long term. Another popular quote from Buffet, "If you aren't willing to own a stock for ten years, don't even think about owning it for ten minutes". In essence, buy a stock as if you were buying a business. Always think in this manner when contemplating a share purchase.

Simple businesses you understand

One of the most important quotes from Warren Buffet is to "never invest in a business you can't understand". If you cannot write what a business does in one sentence you should probably not be buying the shares. As a business owner you want to buy a simple business whose fundamentals you understand. A good starting point is to look up the businesses on your high street or shopping mall or look at the products and services you use regularly. Examples will include utilities, telecommunications, pharmaceuticals, groceries, hotels, fast food, leisure, transport, banking and retailers. Everyday experiences should alert you to business opportunities. For example, as a smart investor you may be prompted to research the shares of your local grocery shop where the aisles are always congested with human traffic and you struggle to find space in the car park.

You may have an edge if you work in a business sector and therefore understand the dynamics and prospects. Professionals can use their knowledge of a particular industry to their advantage. For example, doctors and pharmacists should have a better insight into pharmaceutical companies than a petroleum engineer would. They read the latest research results before anyone else, attend conferences where preliminary data on drugs are presented and have intimate knowledge of the efficacy of new drugs and how they can transform the fortunes of a pharmaceutical company. An orthopaedic surgeon may find a new hip prosthesis from a young company has significant advantages over older models before the stock market does. Surprisingly, these professionals are unlikely to use such unique knowledge to buy the shares when they are available at reasonable prices and usually not until the information is universally known and the share price has appreciated. The doctor is probably busy investing in an obscure oil company in the most far-flung part of the universe instead of the biotechnology company with a potential blockbuster drug. Conversely, the petroleum engineers with a better knowledge of the oil industry will be seeking out the latest biotechnology company to invest in. Buffet advises you "invest within your circle of competence" and that "it's not how big the circle that counts, it's how well you define the parameters". Use your knowledge of an industry to your advantage.

Look for simple businesses, examine and understand their fundamentals, finances and long-term prospects.

Consistent growth

Earnings growth

The long-term investor should look for businesses with a consistent history of growth in sales and earnings over many years. There is no guarantee this consistency will continue in the future but in general such companies tend to outperform those with an erratic earnings history. Invest in businesses whose earnings are likely to be higher in the future. Companies usually publish their 5- or sometimes 10-year financial summary in their annual reports. These are also now freely available on company websites or financial online services such as Digital Look and Business Week. Search for companies where revenues and earnings have grown consistently over the last 5–10 years. From the financial summary you can calculate the long-term average growth of earnings per share (EPS) for the company. This will assist in grouping companies into fast, slow and medium-rate growers. The very fast small growers increase their EPS at 20–25% annually, medium growers 10–12% and the slow growers at less than 10%.

Dividends growth

For dividend-paying companies, look for those with a long history of consistent growth in their dividend payment. Dividend growth and reinvestment, compounded over time, accounts for over 90% of long-term equity returns. So in addition to a reasonable yield, a long history of dividend growth is probably more important.

Dividend cover

Check how much the dividend is covered by earnings from the Consolidated income statement and look for companies with a dividend cover of at least 2. Large cash-generative businesses can comfortably maintain a dividend cover as low as 1.5. Beware of investing below that level.

The rule of 72

You can calculate an approximate estimate of how many years it will take to double your investment by dividing 72 by the percentage rate of growth. The long-term investor should aim to construct a portfolio of growth stocks that will potentially double their investment every 5 years. The rule of 72 calculates this as an average growth rate of about 14.5%. This can be achieved from an earnings growth of 10–12% whilst the remainder accrues from dividend growth.

Financially strong and profitable

This is perhaps the most important consideration for the long-term investor. There is a risk inherent in shares. The investor can reduce this risk by avoiding financially weak companies that could go bankrupt. As a business owner you want to purchase shares in companies that are profitable and financially strong. Invest in companies with strong balance sheets. They are more likely to withstand economic downturns. Companies that are heavily indebted are vulnerable during such periods. When screening companies for investment, the first place to look is the consolidated balance sheet. Check how much cash the company has in relation to debt. Seek out those with an increasing cash pile with little or no debt. Calculate the debt-to-equity ratio or gearing, avoiding those with a net gearing of more than 50%. This is particularly important for small companies. Debt is not always bad when used sensibly to grow shareholder returns. The smart investor, however, reduces the risk of financial disasters by selecting companies with strong balance sheets. As Peter Lynch put it, "never invest in a company without understanding its finances. The biggest losses in stocks come from companies with poor balance sheets". Anthony Bolton admits that his biggest investment losses were nearly always in companies with poor balance sheets and he advises that "if in doubt about how a company is doing, follow the cash". Examine the cash flow statement to ensure the business is generating increasing free cash flow from its activities.

The Z-Score

The Z-Score is a measure of the financial strength of non-financial companies but is not often available to private investors. Published in 1968 by Edward Altman, who was then an assistant professor of finance at New York University, the Z-Score is a statistical formula derived from 5 key financial ratios taken from the profit and loss account and the balance sheet. The lower the score, the greater the probability of the company running into financial distress and going into bankruptcy. In general, the smart investor should avoid companies with a score of less than 1. Scores of more than 2.6 are attractive. The H-Score is a version of the Z-Score that rates the financial strength of companies from 0 to 100, with 100 being the strongest. Companies with a score of less than 25 are best avoided.

Low-cost and efficient businesses

When comparing companies in the same industry, consider those with a high pre-tax profit margin. Businesses with a higher margin have lower operating costs and therefore are able to translate a greater proportion of their sales into profits. You can calculate the profit margins from the consolidated income statement. Low-cost operators with high profit margins are able to withstand economic hardship better than those with a very small margin where deteriorating revenues may tip the business into a loss unless there is a corresponding reduction in costs. There is an in-built culture of efficiency in these low-cost operators that is second nature. They always have an advantage over their less efficient competitors who may be stung into remedial action to lower their operating costs during economic downturns. Also screen for companies with high post-tax returns on shareholder equity, another metric of a profitable business. This is the proportion of the profit attributable to equity holders obtained from the consolidated income statement to the total shareholder equity at the bottom of the consolidated balance sheet. A simple method is to use the average shareholder equity for the previous two years as the denominator.

Excellent long-term prospects – franchise businesses

When looking to invest in a business, it may be worthwhile to ask yourself what will happen to the business if you invested and went to sleep for 50 years. Will the business still be around and, if so, will it be more valuable and profitable than it is today? Invest in businesses where the long-term prospects are favourable and predictable. Many such companies have brand recognition like Coca-Cola, Microsoft, McDonald's, Marks and Spencer and Tesco. Look for companies with a strong competitive advantage and an enduring business franchise. Buffet describes franchise value as a moat around the castle of business. The deeper the moat, the more powerful the protection against the inevitable assault from competitors. He qualifies a franchise company as one with a product or service that is needed, has no close substitute and is not regulated. Such companies enjoy pricing flexibility that allows them to raise prices even when demand is flat and they are able to earn above-average returns on capital. In general, businesses with strong franchises are more likely to make the investor money than those with weak franchises. Gillette and Coca-Cola have been core and permanent holdings in Buffet's portfolio at Berkshire Hathaway.

Beware of earnings based on one new hot product. They usually attract competition and the hot product in no time becomes a cheap commodity item. Also avoid companies where the major proportion of sales is to one buyer. Their prospects are dependent on the whims of the buyer who may switch allegiance to a competitor at short notice.

Reasonable valuation

A fantastic company may not make a good investment if the share price is too expensive. The smart investor should only invest when the price is reasonable to reduce the risk of capital losses.

Some financial ratios are helpful when assessing how cheap or expensive a share price is.

Historical P/E ratio

A simple method to check the valuation of a company is to look at the historical share prices and P/E ratio. These are available from annual reports, company websites and financial websites. For example, Digital Look publishes the 5-year high and low and average P/E for each company and the ratio of the current P/E to the historical average. When available, 10-year historical data are even more valuable as they will show the performance through various business cycles. The smart investor should study and understand the range of normal valuations for the company and the relevant business sector. The P/E ratio will overshoot the mean value either positively or negatively during periods of optimism and pessimism respectively and would tend to revert to a mean value following these extreme excursions. This reversion to mean (RTM) is one of the most valuable lessons for the investor. For Anthony Bolton, "buying when valuations are low against history substantially increases your chance of making money; while buying when they are high increases your risk of loss". The most returns will accrue from investments made when the P/E is well below the historical average. For the smart investor, the relative P/E ratio is therefore more useful than the current absolute value. By purchasing shares when they are selling at valuations significantly below their historical mean, described by Bolton as a "valuation anomaly", the investor has a margin of safety that reduces the downside risk. Such valuation anomalies are more likely to be found among small and medium-sized companies, most of whom attract less research, attention and analysis from brokers and provide an opportunity for the dedicated investor. However, during the recent market downturn in 2007–2008, when all asset classes got hammered, anomalies were evident in the valuations of many large companies as well. There are periods when excellent companies experience a difficult patch; for example, collapse of a subsidiary, accidents or natural disasters. The share price usually plummets. If you understand the company and its long-term fundamentals, investing at this time may be rewarding.

The P/E to growth ratio (PEG)

This is another valuation metric derived by dividing the average annual earnings growth (EPS) into the P/E ratio. A company growing at 10% annually with a P/E of 20 has a PEG of 2, whilst a 20% grower with a P/E of 10 has a PEG of 0.5. Ideally, look to invest in companies with a PEG of less than 1. The further below 1 the better. The investor should understand how the specific PEG ratio for a company has been derived and use it in conjunction with other factors when researching a company. Bolton advises caution when using PEG for valuation. In comparing a company with 5 times earnings growing at 5% a year, another at 10 times earnings growing at 10% and a third at 20 times earnings growing at 20%, all with an attractive PEG of 1, he will always pick the 5% grower. Companies rarely grow at an annual rate of 20% or more for long periods. When the growth rate falters, a corresponding fall in share price occurs.

Peter Lynch describes a formula which I find very useful as a quick valuation guide. Add the dividend yield to the long-term growth rate and divide by the P/E ratio.

(Long-term growth rate + Dividend yield) ÷ P/E ratio

A figure of 2 or more is excellent while less than 1 is poor.

Other useful valuation yardsticks are the price to sales, enterprise value to sales and price to book value ratios.

Price to sales ratio

This is the ratio of the share price to sales or revenue (price to sales ratio or PSR). The PSR is most valuable in comparing companies within the same sector. It is calculated from the ratio of the share price to sales per share as follows:

share price ÷ (sales ÷ no of shares in issue)

Enterprise value to sales ratio

More experienced investors prefer to use the ratio of enterprise value (EV) to sales (EV/S) which strips out the effects of debt. EV is calculated by adding the market capitalisation (share price x number of shares on issue) to debt and subtracting cash. For such investors, the ratio of EV to earnings before interest, taxes, depreciation and amortisation (EV/EBITDA) is a better valuation tool than the P/E ratio.

Price to book ratio (PBR)

The price to book ratio (PBR) is the ratio of the share price to the company net asset value (NAV).

Free cash flow per share

The free cash flow per share, calculated as the cash generated per share divided by the share price, is another valuation ratio for the experienced investor. The free cash flow (FCF) can be calculated from the cash flow statement by subtracting tax and capital expenditure from the operating cash flow. The EV/FCF ratio is very valuable to the experienced investor.

These more difficult ratios may not be particularly useful to the novice investor who should first learn how to calculate and analyse the simpler valuation ratios. However, the smart investor should have an understanding of what they denote, especially when screening and analysing companies in the same business sector. Fortunately, they are freely available from online financial websites and the investor is spared the rigour and ordeal of calculating them.

Develop an investment thesis

Before purchasing a stock, the smart investor should develop and write down an investment thesis for buying the stock. This will be similar to the Peter Lynch's "two-minute drill". He likes to give a two-minute monologue that even a child could understand which covers the reasons for his interest in the stock, what has to happen for the company to succeed and any pitfalls. Having researched a company, the smart investor should be able to write an investment thesis on a single A4 sheet of paper. The information should include key valuation and financial strength ratios. Always include the date the thesis was written as a future reference. Show the maximum price you will be prepared to pay for the shares. This is an example of an investment thesis for Company A, written on January 7, 2009 using figures for the financial year ending December 31, 2007.

> Company A is a cyclical UK company with a history of strong consistent earnings growth. It has withstood the current economic slump, has a strong balance sheet and order book, is selling at a reasonable valuation and has excellent long-term prospects, which will be reflected in significant upside re-grading as the economy improves.
>
> Share price 184.25p; Market capitalisation £163.26m
>
> Revenue: consistent growth over 5 years from £170.15m in 2003 to £300.66m in 2007
>
> Pre-tax profit £38.36m; Profit margin 12.8%
>
> EPS 35.74P; Average 5-year EPS growth 42%
>
> PE 184.25/35.74 = 5.2; PEG 0.1
>
> Dividend 20p; Dividend cover 1.8
>
> Cash 5.45m; Current borrowings £53.50m. No long-term debt. Gearing 25.41%
>
> Return on capital employed (ROCE) 42.31%
>
> PE: 5-year high 14.6; 5-year average PE 12.80; Current PE/average PE = 0.40
>
> Price to pay: EPS x Average 5-year PE = 35.74p x 12.80 = 457p

This analysis indicated a significant margin of safety at the share price of 184.25p. The maximum price of 457p is only a guide based on the current earnings. Ten-year financial figures, if available, provide a more accurate valuation model by revealing a company's performance through an economic cycle.

The investment thesis should be re-checked from time to time. Have the company fundamentals changed? Is the balance sheet still as strong? Is there a major threat to the business, for example from litigation? As long as the fundamentals and investment thesis remain intact, you remain invested. On the contrary, if the fundamentals have seriously deteriorated and especially if there is a significant threat to the company's survival and viability, the smart investor should dispose of the shares even if doing so will incur a loss. The money is better deployed in a more attractive business.

The investor should maintain a list of companies with a strong investment thesis that may be possible future 'buys' and monitor them from time to time. Having an online portfolio of a potential "buy list" of shares is very useful in this respect.

Sensible diversification

One way to minimise the downside risk in your share portfolio is by diversification. This is selection based on market size, industry, growth or yield rate. Companies behave differently in varying economic conditions or in response to mishaps. Since you cannot reliably predict what may happen to the future prospects and earnings of a company, diversification lowers the potential risk. Often some of the biggest gains are made from companies you least expect to provide them. Both winners and losers will emerge from a portfolio of shares. The aim of the smart investor is to pick more winners than losers and employ all available tools to increase the odds of picking winners.

Diversification should be done sensibly and not just for its own sake. Peter Lynch cautions that "a foolish diversity is the hobgoblin of investors". Companies should be picked that meet the investment qualities espoused in this book and certainly after thorough research and at reasonable valuations. A sensible recommendation is to put a third each of your investment in small growth shares, large and medium-sized companies. There is no magic number on how many shares to have in a portfolio as long as they are picked sensibly and the investor can keep tabs on all of them. Too much diversification can be counterproductive. As Warren Buffet argues, "wide diversification is only required when investors do not understand what they are doing" and "diversification may preserve wealth, but concentration builds wealth". A reasonable number of stocks for a small portfolio is 3–10. Quality over quantity is the mantra.

Be a proud shareholder – use the products

The shareholder, who in effect is a part-owner of a business, should be proud to use the company's products and services. You derive some satisfaction in the knowledge that your custom is contributing to the company profits and the dividend you receive. Warren Buffet does not just have Coca-Cola as one of his permanent holdings but his favourite drink is a cherry coke which he is always keen to promote. If you hold shares in Tesco or Marks and Spencer be proud to shop in their stores and promote their products to your friends and family as you would do if it were your personal business. If you own shares in Majestic wines, be a loyal customer. If you are a shareholder in Greggs then be proud to buy their baguettes. If the companies are successful you are rewarded by increasing dividends and rising share prices.

CHAPTER 7

The perfect time to invest

Winning with stocks requires only patience, not foresight.
Jeremy Siegel

The time of maximum pessimism is the best time to buy and the time of maximum optimism is the best time to sell.
John Templeton

Prediction is very difficult, especially if it's about the future.
Niels Bohr

When is the best time to buy shares? Is there a perfect time to invest? Are there different times to buy shares from different business sectors? These are some of the key questions the investor is often confronted with, especially during market downturns when there is considerable fear and anxiety about shares and their prices. A more difficult decision for most investors is deciding when to sell.

Investment trends

Historical trends

Technical analysts use historical share price trends and behaviour to predict when to buy or sell. There are historical calendar trends like the January effect, where share prices tend to rise during January and therefore shares are bought towards the end of the year and sold in the January rally. One explanation for the January effect in the USA where the tax year ends on December 31st is that many investors sell their shares towards the end of year to generate a tax loss and buy them back in January. Another common historical trend predicts that if the first 5 trading days of January are up, the end of January and also the year end are usually up. Share prices tend to fall in September (September effect). Though several market crashes have occurred in the month of October, including 1929, 1987, 1997 and 1998, the October effect in which share prices tend to fall in October is not borne out in reality. In the United States, the presidential election cycle theory suggests that following election of a new president, the stock market declines in the first year and rises in the last three. In the UK, one of the oldest investment adages advises investors to "sell in May and go away. Stay away till St Leger Day". The St Leger horse race is the final classic of the flat racing season usually run in mid-September. The inference is to stay away from the market during the summer. Historically, the majority of stock market gains in both the UK and USA usually occur between November and April. None of these trends is perfect. For example, investors that sold in May 2009 would have missed the 18% gain in the FTSE 100 by St Leger's Day.

Market sentiment

Some investors use the historical pattern of previous bull and bear markets to time their investment decisions. There are several indicators of market sentiment at both extremes of valuation. For the private investor, these include directors' buy to sell ratio of their company shares, the number of new fund launches, brokers' recommendations and indicators of market valuation like P/E ratios, price to book value or free cash flow. A higher proportion of directors buy their company shares when they perceive them to be cheap. Bull markets are characterised by several new fund launches, very optimistic brokers and share valuations in excess of historical averages. The professional investor may also have insight into the "put to call" ratios in the options market, the cash position of investment managers and detailed analysis of market sectors and individual companies.

Economic factors

The timing of investment may be influenced by economic factors. A macro-economic or "top-down" policy uses global factors like the interest rate policy and inflationary trends whilst a micro-economic or "bottom-up" approach will study the outlook for individual companies and industries. Often the market is forward-looking and may not reflect the current economic climate. A bull run may be in progress with the market reaching new highs even when the economy is weak.

Market timing

It is difficult and I dare say impossible to consistently predict the direction of the market or the turning point in business cycles. Even experienced investment professionals and seasoned economists often get it wrong. As a group their record as highly paid "experts" is very poor. It is a useful end of year exercise to review the predictions made by the professionals at the beginning of the year. They predict the likely level of the market index at the year end and select shares that are likely to outperform. Historical trends are not perfect or reliable. If you can accurately forecast the exact turning points in business cycles, buying at the very bottom of the market and selling at the top, this will be the most profitable investment strategy. In reality, nobody can predict these points, which only become apparent with the wonderful benefit of hindsight.

Invest regularly – pound-cost averaging

One way for the smart long-term investor to ignore market timing is to make regular monthly purchases with a set sum. By doing so you employ a strategy called pound-cost averaging (dollar-cost averaging in the USA). For the same amount of money, you get more shares when prices are low and fewer when they are high. Over time you achieve a low average cost per share. This strategy is particularly effective when markets are very volatile and removes the necessity for the investor to judge when prices are relatively high or low. Pound-cost averaging can be used to accumulate a portfolio of shares and is a smart method for purchasing collective funds like unit and investment trusts through low-cost savings plans. The long-term investor is therefore grateful for periods of market depression, which present a wonderful opportunity to purchase more shares in excellent companies and thereby reduce their average cost.

By investing a set sum every month, simplified by using a bank direct debit facility, you are removed from the emotions of timing your investments. You are detached from the constant debate about market and economic cycles. There was fierce debate in 2009 about the likely shape of the economic recovery from the recession – whether it will it be a V, where a sharp fall is followed by a sharp recovery, a W, when recovery is followed by a second downturn, a WW with two double dips or U-shaped where the economy stagnates before recovering. Depending on which recovery was predicted, different shares were recommended for the investor. There was also vigorous debate about the rally in share prices in the summer of 2009 from the market lows reached in late March. Whilst some predicted the start of a new bull market, others cautioned it was a bear rally destined to lure the unwary. Investors were unsure whether to take profits or keep buying. In 2010 there was uncertainty about a double dip recession and whether the economy was heading for a long period of deflation or inflation. The discipline of a monthly investment plan shields the long-term investor from these arguments. You are not influenced by the predictions, debates, controversies and arguments. Equipped with the knowledge that no one can predict the future direction of the economy or market, the smart investor maintains a disciplined and regular monthly investment plan without distraction, allowing the powers of pound-cost averaging, dividend reinvestment and compound interest to work through their portfolio.

Ignore the market

The smart long-term investor should therefore concentrate on finding profitable companies with favourable long-term prospects whose dynamics they understand and on selling at reasonable valuations. Once you find such a company, you should ignore what the market is doing. According to Warren Buffet, "as far as I'm concerned, the stock market doesn't exist. It is there only as a reference to see if anybody is offering to do anything foolish". At the height of markets, most valuations are stretched and it may be difficult to find suitable new investments fulfilling your criteria. Long-term investors should not, however, significantly reduce their holdings no matter how high the market appears. Avoid switching in and out of shares and incurring excessive dealing charges. Invest regularly, reinvest your dividends and remember the power of compound interest.

Avoid the herd instinct

The smart investor must develop a knack for independent thinking and analysis. Learn how to research companies for investment using some of the simple measurements outlined in this book and when you find a business that fulfils those criteria you should have the courage to invest.

Detach yourself from the consensus view and zombie-like investing style that buys the same shares everyone is buying and sells with the masses. The professional fund managers are very likely to launch and recommend new theme funds and shares at the top of the market. Technology shares were the buzz just before they crashed. Likewise, several property, emerging market and commodity funds were being tipped and new ones launched in 2007 and early 2008 just before they bombed. You can almost be certain it is close to the market top when the topic of discussion at the dinner party, doctors' mess or workplace coffee rooms is about shares. The same applies to the property market. We rush out and buy lemming-like when prices are rising and everyone is talking about shares but are very fearful to buy when prices fall to bargain levels and the so-called experts are replete with pessimism.

Beware of hot tips

Likewise avoid investing in the latest "hot tip". A hot tip may form the basis to carry out independent research to see if the company fulfils your investment criteria. Do not speculate and invest blindly based on such a tip. Such trading may be profitable in the short term because the so-called tip is known to a lot more people and the momentum effect may lead to a rise in the share price. If the fundamentals are poor so will the eventual returns be. Similarly, avoid the urge to buy shares first thing on a Monday morning following recommendations in the weekend financial press. The professional market-makers who set prices and read the same media articles will usually raise the share prices and increase the spread between the bid and offer prices on Monday morning knowing that a lot of amateur investors will be clamouring to buy the tips. The share prices will often fall later in the day or over the following days. The speculator sells in a panic at a loss. The only winner is the market-maker. Such a trigger-happy investment style also incurs dealing charges and stamp duty. There are lots of bruised egos and bank balances on Monday mornings. Perhaps to the long list of admonitions for the smart investor should be added, "beware and be fearful of the morning-after Monday market".

Use broker recommendations sensibly

Most professional managers have a short-term horizon in their approach to investment. Shares are bought and sold within a short timescale to produce safe returns and to reflect the consensus view of the investment institution. In the same vein, analysts tend to recommend shares based on short-term considerations. A company with excellent long-term prospects may attract different recommendations from brokers that can change from month to month without any fundamental shift in the company prospects. By thinking independently and long-term, the smart investor may use a contrarian approach at such times to achieve a significant return.

Avoid complacency – follow the story

It is very easy to become complacent and indifferent with your investments, especially during bull markets when most share prices are rising. As a part-owner it is critical you follow the progress of your businesses to ensure the long-term story and therefore the reasons you became an investor remain intact. You should follow the periodic company announcements, any news items about the company and read the annual and interim accounts. Cast your vote on important issues and if you can find the time attend the annual meetings. By being conversant with the business you are more likely to detect when the fundamentals and especially the financial strength are deteriorating. Revisit your investment thesis for each company from time to time to ensure your reasons for investing in the company have not changed. Read the financial pages of newspapers. The *Financial Times* is very useful for the serious investor. If you cannot afford to buy the daily, consider the *FT Weekend* which summarises the week's key business events and has a separate personal financial sector. However, most of the daily newspapers have very good-quality financial pages. On the web, business news is available at Yahoo Finance, Google Finance, FT.com, CNBC, Bloomberg, Reuters, Digital Look and hosts of other sites. On the television, CNBC and Bloomberg are dedicated financial channels.

Stay the course

It is critical the long-term investor stays invested even through market crashes and economic downturns when there is widespread pessimism and fear. As long as you have a long-term investment horizon and the company fundamentals are still sound, these are periods to add to your portfolio. The other reason to invest through the bear market is that when the market changes direction upwards, it can be so sudden and rapid that many investors miss the opportunity. This change in direction tends to occur while the news is still bad. Market cycles are usually out of sync with economic cycles. It is not unusual for share prices to rise strongly while the economy is still in poor shape as the market anticipates future recovery. Several studies show that most of the gains in a bull market occur on only a few days. If you were out of the market on those days, which tend to be at the start of the new trend, your returns will be considerably eroded. Any investor who was waiting on the sidelines following the market lows of March 2009 would have missed the strong market rally of July 2009 when the FTSE 100 index had its best monthly performance for 6 years, rising by 8.5% to end the month at 4608.32.

When to sell

Investors tend to have more difficulty deciding when to sell. For the smart long-term investor, the answer is simple and straightforward – very rarely. For Warren Buffet, "my favourite time frame for holding a stock is forever".

There are 3 reasons why Anthony Bolton will sell a share: "if something negates the investment thesis; if it meets my valuation target; or if I find something better". However, remember he was a fund manager. The principles are the same but the private long-term investor has a different agenda. If the business fundamentals and investment thesis are still intact you should seldom have cause to sell. The most compelling reason for the long-term investor to sell is because of changing business fundamentals. Be alert to a slowing earnings growth or signs of a deteriorating balance sheet when the company has taken on too much debt or where inventories are accumulating rapidly. Also, declining profit margins may be a reflection of rising costs or increasing competition. The slump in prospects may be due to a poorly performing subsidiary or a new product. Be cautious when management embarks on grandiose acquisitions or expansion. Very often these acquisitions are done to satisfy the ego of the management and in most cases they destroy shareholder value. The disastrous acquisition of ABN AMRO by the Royal Bank of Scotland is a case in point. The best way for most companies to use excess cash is either to return it to shareholders by increased dividends or to buy back shares. Sensible acquisitions made at reasonable valuations can be rewarding. Growing companies often reinvest a greater proportion of their earnings in the business. This is beneficial when the reinvestment enhances earnings and leads to a corresponding appreciation of shareholder equity. Also be wary of managers with very expensive tastes in lavish headquarters and corporate jets. Where management values appear not to be aligned with those of the shareholders, the smart investor should consider selling. Avoid emotional attachment to a stock and never fall in love with a share. Quoting Buffet again, "a stock doesn't know that you own it". Where the company fundamentals deteriorate to such a degree that your assessment advises you to sell, the smart investor should dispose of the shares, even if doing so incurs a loss.

Remember that most of the long-term returns from the stock market derive from compounding reinvested dividends. This is a powerful phenomenon that gathers momentum the longer the investment horizon and is perhaps the strongest argument for investing for the long haul and staying invested. The frequent buying and selling of shares most often leads to poor returns. One of the reasons is the cost involved in such erratic trading. In addition to the commission paid for each buy and sell order, there is also stamp duty for each share purchase – currently 0.5% in the UK. It follows that each time you buy shares you immediately generate a loss because of these costs. The share price has to appreciate significantly to overcome this deficit before you make a profit.

There is an argument that it is never wrong to take a profit. There is therefore a temptation to realise profits when share prices are high. Some experts advise selling half your shares when they double in price so you get your principal back. At such times it is useful to remember that it is a mistake to assume that because a share price has doubled it cannot do so again. Quality growth companies can go higher. Re-check and follow the story. As long as the fundamentals and investment thesis remain favourable, hold on for the long run. Remember as well that when you sell, you have to find a better investment for the money raised. Not uncommonly it is invested in a lower-quality asset with poorer returns.

Another common suggestion is to sell when the P/E ratio is above the historical average for the company because of the compelling evidence of reversion to mean. This implies that the investor is spotting the top of the share price cycle. The investor should be aware that in bull markets, momentum investing can carry the share price way beyond the previous high. The cautious investor may decide to sell if their valuation target has been met. It is rare to get your timing right and sell at the very top of the market but you hope to be close.

Conversely there is often an urge to sell either because the share price has been relatively static or, more commonly, fallen significantly. The long-term investor has to be patient when the prices of quality companies appear not to reflect the fundamentals. Over time share prices will appreciate in step with the growth in earnings. When prices are low, focus on the underlying business fundamentals. Is the investment thesis still strong? Are the shares selling at a significant discount to value? Is the company still financially strong with little prospect of bankruptcy? Long-term investors are delighted during such periods of rare buying opportunity to reduce the average cost of investment in quality companies. During severe economic downturns, the prices of almost all companies are savagely beaten down. The smart investor should boldly deploy pound-cost averaging to pick up discounted quality companies. According to Peter Lynch, "if you can't convince yourself 'When I'm down 25 percent, I'm a buyer' and banish forever the fatal thought 'When I'm down 25 percent, I'm a seller', then you'll never make a decent profit in stocks". However, do not buy a company with poor fundamentals because the price appears cheap. A share price that has lost 90% of its value can lose 100%. The experience of Northern Rock and Bradford Bingley investors is instructive.

An investor might have to sell to meet an obligation like purchasing a house, paying for a child's education or for tax reasons. For the investor approaching retirement, wealth preservation should be of paramount importance. It may be sensible for the smart investor to realise some gains from a share portfolio and increase the proportion of assets allocated to fixed income investments bonds and cash. The investor nearing retirement is usually advised to have 20–40% of their assets in cash.

CHAPTER 8

What about the economy?

Stop trying to predict the direction of the stock market, the economy, interest rates, or elections.

Warren Buffet

Economic cycles

The global economy behaves in a cyclical fashion, alternating between periods of growth and prosperity that are followed by slumps and depression. The rate and extent of this cyclic trend varies between nations and geographical regions. The stock markets similarly go through bull runs with rising share prices and considerable optimism, followed by downturns with falling or stagnant prices, fear and pessimism. However, the smart investor should have a simplistic view of economic cycles. This is particularly useful when widespread pessimism abounds and doom prophets predict the end of the world. During economic recessions as we have recently experienced, the investor should keep the bigger picture in perspective. The world is certainly not coming to an end. The long-term trend for the global economy is for growth, increasing prosperity and great technological advances. The world population and global demographics are growing, not falling. Life expectancies are generally longer and improving. International trade and commerce are expanding. More people will require food, clothing, shelter, pharmaceutical products, healthcare, telecommunications, transport, banking and leisure activities. It therefore follows that when asset prices are slashed during economic downturns, the smart investor should be emboldened to be aggressive in buying at discounted values. The best time for the long-term investor to be buying is when there is blood on the streets as the saying goes, with stock screens flashing red, the end of the world is predicted to be just round the corner and spellbinding fear abounds. If you view the economy with the long-term prospects in mind, you will not be panicked into selling your holdings. Think long-term and ignore the headlines. Stock markets will recover. Another bull run will appear as investors chase up rising prices creating a new momentum. History tends to repeat itself and will reward the smart long-term investor.

The smart investor will understand how economic cycles affect the prospects and therefore the viability and profitability of different business sectors. The fortunes of cyclical sectors like property, miners and financials mirror the ups and downs of the economic cycle. They are best bought during recessions or downturns when their prices are usually beaten down. Some other sectors have more defensive qualities with more stable earnings from year to year. These include pharmaceuticals, tobacco and utilities. They tend to underperform during upswings in the economic cycle as investors chase recovering cyclical shares. The contrarian investor is presented with a useful buying opportunity.

Regional trends

The smart investor should also be conscious of regional economic trends and themes. With increasing prosperity and disposable personal incomes, the economies of China, Brazil, India, Russia and the Asian tigers like Indonesia, Taiwan, South Korea, Hong Kong, Singapore, Malaysia and the Philippines are growing at a considerably faster rate than the more developed Western economies. A report by PricewaterhouseCoopers in 2008 projects that the economies of the 7 emerging markets of China, India,

Brazil, Mexico, Indonesia and Turkey, referred to as E7, will be 50% larger than the current G7 economies by 2050. The G7 is made up of Canada, France, Germany, Italy, Japan, USA and the UK. The Chinese economy is predicted to overtake the USA in about a decade while India will have done so by 2050.

These economies of the future are undergoing rapid industrialisation. They tend to have more volatile stock markets and consequently carry higher investment risk. The argument that their prospects are decoupled from Western economies was not borne out during the recent recession when they all fell in unison. The amount invested in emerging markets will depend on your attitude to risk, balanced against the potential returns. The smart investor should probably allocate 10–15% of their portfolio to these high-growth economies. Exposure can be gained through a specialist broad-based emerging markets fund. Individual country funds are generally riskier. Alternatively one can invest indirectly through the UK companies that conduct a large part of their business in these countries. Examples include HSBC and Standard Chartered banks. Several others like Tesco are also expanding their international footprint.

A 2009 *Fortune* article was titled "It's China's world. We just live in it". China is experiencing phenomenal industrial growth of its export-led economy. It has a growing foreign exchange reserve that is estimated at over $2.4 trillion in June 2010 and needs enormous amounts of natural resources to power this economic boom. The diversified portfolio of the smart investor should generally have some exposure to commodities either through exchange traded funds (ETFs) or diversified companies like Rio Tinto and BHP Billiton.

Technology trends

The smart investor can also profit from following technological trends and investing in champion companies. We have had the era of computers and great companies like Microsoft and Intel. The mobile phone boom produced stars like Nokia and Vodafone. More recently smartphones are creating a wave led by Apple which, in addition to the very popular iPhone, makes the iconic iPod, Mac computers and the iPad tablet, and Samsung with the Galaxy phones and tablets. Online advertising has overtaken television and paper advertising in popularity and growth and here the unquestionable star is Google. Social networking and social media have changed the way we interact with each other and how businesses promote their products. Facebook, Twitter and LinkedIn are the major players. Keep abreast of these economic trends, positioning your portfolio to take full advantage.

Ecommerce

Another economic trend to follow is the increasing popularity of ecommerce and online services. The dominant players include international giants like Amazon, the biggest ecommerce business, and eBay, the online auction site. The UK has profitable companies like Moneysupermarket.com for financial services, Rightmove.com where estate agents and developers advertise homes for sale or rent and ASOS the fashion retailer. In addition many traditional "bricks and mortar" businesses including the major supermarkets and retailers like Next, Argos – part of the Home Retail Group – and Tesco are boosting their online enterprises. The UK online retail market hit £78 billion in 2012, growing at an annual rate of about 14%. It is predicted that a third of UK retail sales will be done online by 2022, rising from the current 10%.

CHAPTER 9

Stock screening

It's far better to buy a wonderful company at a fair price than a fair company at a wonderful price.

Warren Buffett

Risk comes from not knowing what you're doing.

Warren Buffet

I don't want a lot of good investments; I want a few outstanding ones. If the job has been correctly done when a common stock is purchased, the time to sell it is almost never.

Philip Fisher

The smart investor should develop a method of screening for companies that meet critical valuation yardsticks. Armed with knowledge of key fundamental valuation metrics, the investor searches the market for suitable companies. An individual company that has aroused interest can be studied in more detail. The internet has made such searches very simple and accessible, with several online sites providing a free service. In the past the serious investor would have had to pore over company reports in a library and manually perform the required quantitative analysis. Financial websites like Digital Look, FT.com, Business Week, and Adfn.com now publish detailed company financial information, including all the important valuation ratios required for screening. The investor is truly spoilt for choice and needs to try a few websites before settling on one or two favourites. I find the screening tools on Digital Look and

FT.com particularly useful. Valuable USA sites include RiskGrades and the Google Stock Screener.

Several strategies can be employed in stock screening. You can screen the whole market or market sectors like the FTSE 100, FTSE 250, small capitalisation index and the techMARK index of technology companies. Alternatively one can screen the companies that make up a business sector like pharmaceuticals, software, real estate, retailers or banks for example. Another strategy is to look for companies based on their fundamentals like earnings growth or dividend yield. The investor may, for example, be interested in companies with an average EPS growth of 15% or increasing dividend payments well covered by earnings for the last 5–10 years.

Fundamental financial ratios and statistics employed in screening include EPS growth, operating margins, return on capital employed (ROCE), PE ratio, PE to growth ratio (PEG), price to sales ratio (PSR), price to book ratio (PBR), cash position, cash flow and gearing, dividend yield, dividend growth and cover. Information is also available on share price performance, analysts' forecasts, broker recommendations, director share dealings and company risk ratings. The investor selects the desired investment parameters and is provided with a list of companies that satisfy the search criteria. These companies then form the basis for more detailed study and research which may include visiting the company website from where financial statements can be downloaded. While you can request a hard copy of the financial reports directly from the company, the internet has made this almost irrelevant.

The smart investor should have some knowledge of company statistics and valuation yardsticks to understand and employ screening strategies. It is not difficult to learn simple fundamental statistics as provided in Chapter 2. This knowledge equips the investor with the tools for independent research and investment. It is invaluable in developing an investment thesis and in picking stocks for the long run.

CHAPTER 10

Low-cost share dealing

The miracle of compounding returns is overwhelmed by the tyranny of compounding costs.

John Bogle

The greatest enemies of the equity investor are expenses and emotions.

Warren Buffet

To quote John Bogle, "costs matter". They do to a very large degree. In building a portfolio, the smart and intelligent investor should be obsessive about keeping expenses to the barest minimum. Avoiding excessive erratic trading is fundamental. This can also be partly achieved through low-cost investment schemes. Competition in the industry means there are numerous low-cost or discount brokers to choose from.

Nominee accounts

The majority of share purchases are now done through nominee accounts. These are electronic accounts in which the shares are held collectively in the name of the broker but the client has beneficial ownership. The nominee deals with all settlements, corporate actions and collection of dividends. They provide low dealing charges, quicker settlement and usually allow for reinvestment of dividends. The major disadvantage is that by having the shares in the nominee's name, the investor is deprived of certain shareholder rights like company reports and voting rights. Often company perks are not available to shareholders in nominee accounts. You can request paper certificates but these have become increasingly expensive to hold.

Share dealing services

There are several competitive low-cost share dealing services. Most offer a telephone service but the cheapest deals are online and can be as low as £8 per deal. Several allow share dealing in sterling on foreign stock markets, usually in Europe and the USA. No stamp duty is payable on those markets though the dealing charges may be slightly higher. The smart investor, having done the necessary homework, only needs a low-cost online execution-only share dealing account. They are known as execution-only services because they provide no investment advice, leaving the investor responsible for choosing what funds or shares to buy or sell. Some of the popular stockbrokers include Halifax, Barclays, Selftrade, Hargreaves Lansdown, TD Direct Investing, Iweb Sharedealing and E*TRADE.

Beware of low dealing charges that are only available if you carry out a minimum number of trades in a calendar month. The charges can be as low as £5.95 but you have to trade at least 20 times in the month to qualify. Excessive trading for the small investor is likely to result in poor returns from the cumulative dealing costs.

Regular investment plans

An innovative low-cost share dealing service that I am particularly fond of is the regular investment plans offered by some stockbrokers including Halifax, TD Direct Investing, Selftrade and the Share Centre. They aggregate funds from all investors and make a bulk purchase on set days a month for between £1 and £2 per deal including VAT. They are simple, low-cost and flexible plans that allow for regular pound-cost averaging investment without worrying about market timing. They are especially recommended to the novice investor or one with limited funds who can build a portfolio of shares through a regular monthly investment. They will also appeal to the more experienced and higher net worth investor. For the small investor, purchasing shares monthly through the traditional share dealing services can be expensive. For example if you plan to invest £100 monthly, a commission of £8 for each trade immediately puts you 8% behind. There is also 0.5% stamp duty on share purchases in the UK plus the spread (the difference between purchase and selling price). This significant loss has to be recouped before you show any investment gains. The regular investment plans with their low commissions are therefore well suited to the small investor.

The only disadvantage of these schemes is that the investor does not choose the purchase price. Shares are bought at prices prevailing on the set day. For the long-term investor employing the benefit of pound-cost averaging this is perhaps not of serious consequence.

With the Halifax ShareBuilder account for example, which is an execution-only service, you set up an online regular investment plan from as little as £20 per month by direct debit which is invested on a set day each month. You can choose from four set days each month and pick what shares to invest in. All customer orders are grouped together and cost savings are reflected in a commission of only £2. You can select any number of shares and invest as little as £5 in each. The investor can vary the sum of money or company invested each month and also elect to reinvest all dividends. The investor thereby benefits from pound-cost averaging and the compounding of dividends over time. Dividends can otherwise be left to accumulate in the account and added to the monthly purchase plan or transferred to your bank account. The same regular investment plan can be applied to the Halifax Self-Select Stock and Shares ISA.

Low-cost Individual Savings Account (ISA)

The UK government introduced the Individual Savings Account in 1999 to encourage savings and investments in the stock market free from capital gains tax. In addition, higher-rate taxpayers are exempt from additional tax on dividends. Initially known as Personal Equity Plans (PEPs), they have undergone several transformations. Since April 2008, any individual over the age of 18 can invest a maximum of £7200 in shares each tax year. Of this, £3600 can be held in a cash ISA and transferable into a stocks and shares ISA. This ISA limit is increased annually in line with inflation. The allowance was increased from April 6, 2014 to £11,880 and the cash element to £5940. From July 2014 ISAs will be simplified with the creation of the 'New ISA' (NISA) which will increase the annual limit to £15000, all of which can be invested in a Cash ISA. Investors can also transfer their Stocks and Shares ISA to a Cash ISA.

Eligible investments for an ISA wrapper include stocks and shares, funds and bonds (both government and corporate bonds if they are 5 years from maturity). Previously, companies listed on the Alternative Investment Market (Aim) were ineligible but this restriction was removed from August 5, 2013. From April 28 2014, the 0.5% stamp duty was abolished for Aim share purchases. Investors receive dividends net of 10% tax levied on all stock dividends in the UK. ISAs are therefore particularly attractive to higher-rate tax payers who otherwise pay an extra tax on their dividends.

Many ISA schemes have very high administration charges that are likely to affect the long-term returns. Several brokers have low-cost ISA regular investment plans in nominee accounts as described above that aggregate all funds for investment on set days of the month. The smart investor should employ such low-cost and tax-efficient regular purchase schemes to maximise their returns and also elect to reinvest all dividends.

Chapter 11

Low-cost collective funds

Most individual investors would be better off in an index mutual fund.

Peter Lynch

99% of fund managers demonstrate no evidence of skill whatsoever.

William Bernstein

Investors who find investing in individual shares too risky or are unable to undertake the fundamental analysis required to pick stocks can use a collective fund to invest in the stock market. Collective funds can also form the core of a diversified portfolio for the experienced investor. They are particularly useful as a vehicle to invest in foreign markets. They provide access to the economic growth of emerging countries where investment in individual company shares may be risky and expensive for the UK investor.

With collective funds, professional managers pool together money from many investors and invest in shares, bonds and other assets like property, and money market instruments. They can invest in different geographical areas and market sectors and by holding a large number of shares they reduce the volatility and risk of holding individual shares. The investor should understand the risk profile of these funds before making a commitment. They have a varying degree of risk. For example, funds investing in emerging markets or small companies are considered a higher risk than perhaps one invested in large blue chip UK companies. Several funds can be used to build a diversified portfolio.

Traditionally there have been two major types of collective funds in the UK known as unit trusts and investment trusts. Exchange-traded funds are relatively new but have grown considerably in popularity.

Unit trusts

Also known as mutual funds in the USA, unit trusts are investments where the fund manager purchases shares in different companies, usually 50–100, which are pooled together in a fund. Investors are allocated "units" in the fund. The value of each unit is equivalent to the market value of the underlying investments divided by the number of units on issue. As the share prices of the underlying investments rise, so does the value of each unit. Some unit trusts pay a dividend from the collective dividends received from the shares in the fund. The number of units fluctuates as investors buy and sell them and therefore unit trusts are also known as "open-ended" funds. There is an initial charge to buy unit trusts which is reflected in a different buying and selling price known as the bid/offer spread. You buy at the offer price and sell at the bid price, which is usually lower than the offer price.

Investment trusts

Investment trusts also pool together investors' funds but, unlike unit trusts, they are companies in their own right and are therefore traded on the stock market. Since they have a fixed number of shares on issue they are also known as "closed-ended" funds. Due to the forces of supply and demand the share price may be higher (premium) or lower (discount) than the value of the underlying investments in the fund known as the net asset value (NAV). Unlike unit trusts, these "closed-ended funds" do not have to sell the underlying shares to meet large investor redemptions and therefore tend to have stable long-term investments. Another significant difference from unit trusts is that investment trusts can borrow money to purchase further investments. Known as gearing, this can boost returns in a rising market leading to long-term outperformance. Some funds pay regular dividends collected from the invested shares. Investment trusts can keep 15% of their annual income as reserves, which allows them to smooth out their dividend payments. This is another advantage they hold over unit trusts which do not reserve any part of their income. Like unit trusts, there is a bid/offer price spread.

Total expense ratio (TER)

Collective funds attract an initial charge on purchase, reflected in the bid/offer spread. This can be as high as 5.25% for unit trusts when purchased directly or from commission-based financial advisers. In addition there is an annual management charge which is deducted from the fund. The average is about 1.5% but may be as high as 1.75%. Funds also incur charges when they buy and sell shares within the fund and pay custodial fees for the shares. All these costs make up the total expense ratio (TER), which is often as high as 2% for unit trusts. While funds with low initial and annual charges may not outperform those with higher charges, to achieve the same return, a fund with higher charges has to outperform significantly. High TERs can be a drag on performance and adversely affect the long-term returns from a fund. The common sense and smart investor must critically review and understand the charges levied by a collective fund before making a long-term commitment.

Ongoing charge ratio (OCR)

Following European legislation, funds are now using the ongoing charge instead of the TER. It is similar to the TER, but does not include any performance fee which, together with any transaction costs, are disclosed separately by the fund manager.

Management performance

The rationale for the high charges levied by active unit trust fund managers is based on the premise that they pick stocks that would outperform an index or benchmark. Investors therefore expect such active funds to outperform their passive counterparts that replicate an index or benchmark and do not have an active stock-picking manager. This unfortunately is not the case. Over two thirds of all active funds fail to beat the market, and the odds of finding a fund manager who will consistently beat the market are very much stacked against the investor. A few star managers have excellent long-term records of beating the market. In the UK Anthony Bolton of Fidelity has the most impressive record. Investing £1000 in the Special Situations Fund at its launch in 1979 was worth more than £125,000 27 years later – a 125-fold increase – at a compounded growth rate of more than 20% per annum and 7% per annum above the FTSE All-Share index. In the USA, during his time at the Fidelity Magellan Fund between 1977 and 1990, Peter Lynch achieved an annual return of 29%. Over the 13 years, an investment of $10,000 would have grown to $288,000. Of the current crop of UK managers, Neil Woodford has had stellar performance with the Invesco Perpetual High Income and Income funds. The former returned 104% over 5 years to the end of 2008, over 20% better than its competitors. The 10-year average annual total return to March 2012 was 8.7%, which mirrors Neil Woodford's annualised total return of 9% across his funds over 12 years. These are the exceptional managers. The average performance is otherwise below par and as a group these poorly performing funds are the very ones likely to be recommended by financial advisers who were paid commissions of up to 3% for doing so.

Low-cost strategies

Costs are crucial to long-term investment returns. The smart investor must critically examine and understand the cost structure of a fund before making an investment. The three common sense low-cost strategies will be to invest in a tracker fund, an investment trust with a low expense ratio especially through a savings plan or an exchange traded fund (ETF).

Tracker (Index) funds

Tracker funds, usually unit trusts, are passive collective funds designed to mirror the performance of a particular index like the FTSE All-Share, FTSE 100 and S&P 500. They may buy every stock in an index or use statistical methods to construct a portfolio of shares that replicates the index, known as the "sampling" method. Unlike active funds where the managers buy and sell shares regularly in an attempt to outperform the market and in the process rack up dealing costs, the turnover in tracker funds is minimal and accounts for their low cost. In addition, they have low annual management charges, typically 0.5% but sometimes up to 1%. They usually do not pay commission to intermediaries, another contributing factor to their low cost, and so were unlikely to be recommended to the small investor. Commission payment was abolished in the UK from January 2013. The smart investor, with the ability to undertake independent study, does not need an independent financial adviser who would be likely to recommend an expensive commission-paying actively managed fund. Some active funds may outperform such passive investment but the average active manager fails to do so. Primarily as a result of charges, over the long term, there is a staggering difference in the returns, with the average index fund beating over 75% of active funds.

As an example, consider £1000 invested each in a low-cost tracker fund and the average active unit trust that both grow at a compound annual rate of 7%. The combination of initial and annual charges will reduce the net annual return on the unit trust to about 4.5% while the tracker with no initial charge and an annual charge of 0.5% will achieve a net return of 6.5%. This translates into a return after 10 years of £1553 for the unit trust and £1877 for the index fund – a difference of £324. Over 20 years the unit trust would have grown to £2412 and the tracker to £3524 – a difference of £1112. This illustrates both the power of long-term compound returns and the significant effect of a small difference in charges on the long-term returns. Do not ignore charges.

In the United States, John Bogle, founder of the Vanguard funds, is the major advocate of index funds. He gave a lecture in 2005 titled "the relentless rules of humble arithmetic" in which he showed that between 1983 and 2003 the S&P 500 (a USA stock market index based on the market capitalisations of 500 leading public companies) averaged an annual return of 13%. After deducting 3% for management charges and poor performance, 3.7% for bad timing by investors and 3% for inflation, the average fund only returned 3.3% a year. An average S&P index fund by contrast would have returned 9.8% annually – almost 3 times the real return of the average mutual fund. In addition to charges, this illustrates the destructive effect of poor timing on long-term returns. Investors tend to flock late to shares at the peak of bull markets and sell in panic during downturns with consequent poor returns.

Even among tracker funds charges vary. There is no reason to pay more for a tracker fund if there is a cheaper alternative from a reputable fund manager. Some of the cheapest UK All-Share tracker funds as at March 2013 include the HSBC FTSE All-Share index fund with an annual management charge of 0.25% and a TER of 0.27% and the Fidelity MoneyBuilder UK fund with an annual charge of 0.1% and TER of just 0.3%. The Virgin Money All-Share tracker by comparison has an annual charge of 1% whilst the biggest, the Legal and General UK index fund, has an annual charge of 0.4%. In 2009 Vanguard, the US group, launched low-cost index tracker funds in the UK with charges as low as 0.1%. They are more suited to the large investor as they demand a minimum investment of £100,000 if you go direct. Lower sums can be invested through some discount fund supermarkets including Alliance Trust Savings and Hargreaves Lansdown.

In general it is sensible to choose funds with a TER of less than 0.3.

Investment trust savings plans

Investment trusts tend to have lower costs than unit trusts and are more suited to the small investor. Their average TER is about 1.4%, while about a third have TERs below 1%. I have been a fan of investment trusts over the years. They have not been as popular as the more expensive unit trusts, primarily because financial advisers were paid commission for promoting unit trusts. Indeed many of these advisers and fund managers had investment trusts in their personal portfolios whilst selling their commission-clad expensive cousins to the private investor.

Over the longer term, investment trusts have significantly outperformed unit trusts. A Money Observer report in

October 2009 using Morningstar data showed that of 51 investment trusts with a track record of more than 30 years, 35 (68%) beat the FTSE All-Share index total return of 2367% over the 30 years from October 1979. Of 82 unit trusts, only 23 (28%) beat the index. This is most likely due to their longer-term investment focus, lower fees and ability to use gearing. Investment trusts are particularly attractive when they are trading at a discount to their net asset value.

Many investment trusts have monthly savings plans – a low-cost route through which small investors can gradually build up a sizeable portfolio. For example, you can invest a minimum of £50 monthly or a lump sum of £500 in the Foreign & Colonial Private Investment Plan at a dealing charge of only 0.2% plus stamp duty of 0.5%. An annual charge of £40 plus VAT was introduced in early 2013 which may affect the long-term performance and attractiveness of the funds, especially in small accounts. There is a choice of 13 investment trusts including the Foreign & Colonial Investment Trust (FCIT), the oldest investment trust established in 1868. FCIT has a diversified international portfolio of more than 490 companies in 29 countries and has a compounded long-term total return of 8.0% per annum (9.5% in the 10 years to 2012). Dividends have compounded at 9.3% per annum over the same 10-year period and increased every year since 1970. The OCR in 2013 was 0.9%. F & C Savings Plans can also be used for ISA, pension, child trust fund and children's investment planning.

By their ability to keep 15% of their annual income as reserves, investment trusts can smooth out their dividend payments. Many of them have a strong track record of annual increments in their dividend payout. According to the Association of Investment Companies (AIC), investment trusts with over a 40-year record of dividend increases include City of London Investment Group, Alliance Trust,

Bankers Investment Trust and Caledonia Investments. The City of London Investment Trust, formed in 1860 and incorporated in 1891, increased its dividend for the 46th consecutive year in 2012. It has an OCR of 0.45% and the yield was 3.9% in July 2013. These investment trust dividend stars have rewarded the long-term investor and are excellent core portfolio holdings.

A low-cost monthly savings plan is ideal for the small long-term investor and especially for those who want to avoid the risks inherent in individual shares.

Exchange traded funds (ETFs)

Exchange traded funds are investment vehicles that combine the diversity of a unit trust by holding a portfolio of assets like shares, bonds and alternative investments including currencies and commodities with the flexibility of being traded like shares on the stock market similar to investment trusts. They are increasing in popularity due in large part to their added advantage of low cost. They are designed to track an index like the FTSE 100 and S&P 500, a sector or asset class like commodities, hedge funds, currencies and infrastructure. They provide a route to asset classes or markets that may not be normally accessible to the private investor. ETFs aim to replicate the returns of the underlying market and usually trade as close as possible to the net asset value of the underlying assets. To achieve this, they match the holdings that constitute the index.

There are two main types of ETFs – cash-based and swap-based. Cash-based ETFs, like tracker funds, buy all the shares in the index. Swap-based ETFs, on the other hand, are more complex. They use financial instruments called derivatives to replicate the index. This involves an agreement with another institution, called the counterparty, which provides a return based on the underlying index.

Hence swap-based ETFs carry an extra risk from failure or collapse of the counterparty.

For investors interested in commodities, there are exchange traded commodities (ETCs) which can provide exposure to individual commodities like gold, silver and crude oil or a group of commodities like agriculture, energy and livestock. The smart investor should be careful when investing and differentiate between funds that hold the underlying commodity and swap-based ETCs that carry counterparty risk. For example, ETFs securities Physical Gold, Physical Silver, Physical Platinum and Physical Palladium ETCs are all backed by the relevant physical metal. ETFs Natural Gas on the other hand is swap-based.

Professional managers are exploiting the growing popularity of ETFs to develop more complex products like leveraged and short ETFs. Leveraged ETFs aim to multiply the returns of a given index. For example, a 2% rise may be offered for every 1% rise in an index (2 x leveraged ETF). The investor will also bear a double loss if the index falls. Short ETFs aim to make money when an index falls. They may offer a 2% rise for every fall of 1% (2 x short ETF). If, however, the market rises, the investor loses 2% for every 1% rise. It is obvious these are riskier products suited to the more experienced investor who fully understands the involved risks. They are best avoided by the smart amateur investor who should stick to the simple transparent ETFs.

A major advantage of ETFs is their low cost. The average TER for equity ETFs is about 0.5% but can be as low as 0.15%. In the UK, ETFs are exempt from the 0.5% stamp duty levied on purchasing shares. iShares is a leading ETF brand in the UK, purchased by the investment firm Blackrock from Barclays Global Investors in 2009. The iShares FTSE 100, iShares FTSE 250 and iShares S&P 500, which track the corresponding indices, all have a TER of

0.4% whilst the iShares Corporate Bond fund has a TER of 0.2%. The HSBC FTSE 100 ETF has a TER of 0.35% and the Credit Suisse FTSE 100 a TER of 0.33%. Both hold all the shares in the index. ETFs can be held in an ISA.

The amateur investor is more likely to use ETFs to track an equity index like the FTSE 100 as the core of a portfolio. Specialist ETF funds can be added as satellite investments.

As with investment trusts, independent financial advisers were unlikely to recommend non-commission-paying low-cost ETFs to private investors prior to the banning of commission payments for selling savings plans from the end of 2012. Advisers will instead charge customers a fee. There is increasing awareness and debate about the underlying cost of investment products in general. The simplicity, low cost and scope of the majority of ETFs have made them increasingly popular with investors.

CHAPTER 12

Asset allocation

Diversify your investments.

John Templeton

The smart investor should diversify the risk in their portfolio by holding different asset classes. The choice includes cash, bonds, commodities, private equity, real estate and equities quoted on a public stock market. There is no uniform agreement on how the investor should allocate capital to each asset class. Asset allocation is primarily dictated by the long-term expected returns as determined by personal investment objectives and also significantly by an individual's attitude to risk.

Strategic and tactical asset allocation

Strategic asset allocation (SAA) applies to the spread of investments to the different assets. Tactical asset allocation (TAA) involves the short-term adjustment of a portfolio to take care of imbalances and relative valuations. For example, an asset class with a 15% portfolio weighting may appreciate to 40%. TAA dictates selling some of the asset to rebalance the portfolio. This rebalancing exercise can be carried out annually when, for instance, gains from an equity portfolio are reinvested into cash, bonds or commodities. Whilst SAA sets the long-term objectives, TAA achieves short-term modifications and fine-tuning.

Asset allocation and lifestyling

The decision on asset allocation is primarily based on a triad of factors – an investor's investment objectives, the amount of risk the investor is prepared to take and the investment time horizon. The traditional advice is for the young investor to tilt their allocation towards the riskier end of the spectrum by investing mostly in equities. The longer investment period allows the investor to enjoy the miracle of compounding returns and time to recover from market downturns. The equity allocation is reduced as the investor approaches retirement. For example a 30-year-old may allocate 80% to stocks and 20% to bonds, real estate and other asset classes (80/20 split). A 60/40 asset split in favour of equities seems to be a popular, less aggressive recommendation. The long-term aggressive investor is likely to have 100% of their investment in equities over a 30-year holding period. The converse will be applicable to a 60-year-old as the balance is shifted towards retirement to lower-risk bonds and cash. It is, however, worthwhile to note that with increasing longevity, a 60-year-old investor may have another 20–30 years to live off their investment returns. Similarly, a family saving to purchase a house may invest entirely in cash equivalents. Bonds and cash make very poor long-term investments. They may perform well in the short term but historically equities are the best hedge against inflation and should command a major position in a long-term diversified portfolio.

Correlation and diversification

The smart investor must have a common sense approach to diversification. Some thought should be given to the construction of a diversified equity portfolio. The basis is to pick shares from different sectors that have a poor correlation with each other. Their share prices do not therefore behave in the same manner, thereby reducing the risk and volatility in the portfolio. The same economic event may result in rising share prices in one industry while those in an un-correlated business may fall. For example, the share prices of GlaxoSmithKline and Astra Zeneca, both pharmaceutical companies, tend to react in the same manner to industry-specific events. A portfolio in which they both constitute a significant holding may suffer heavy losses if there is negative news for the pharmaceutical industry. The same is true of Tesco and Sainsbury's, two supermarkets. Diversify by investing in companies in different businesses.

A diversified portfolio will also have some exposure to global equities. However, the smart investor should tread carefully when considering overseas markets, many of which carry significant risk. Emerging markets in particular are touted as being decoupled from the UK market. However, the reality is that most markets show very close correlation, as demonstrated by the universal slump in global markets in 2008 when they all tumbled like a pack of cards. Often they are riskier than UK shares. The investor should have a diversified core of UK shares or funds, with emerging markets limited to about 10% of a portfolio. The proportion will obviously be determined by an investor's attitude to risk. Another factor which may influence investing overseas is the absence of UK equivalents in some niche sectors like technology where companies like Microsoft, Google, Apple and Facebook may appeal to some investors. International exposure may be gained indirectly by investing in UK companies that conduct a major part of their business abroad, for example Vodafone, GlaxoSmithKline, BP, Shell, Tesco, HSBC and Standard Chartered Bank.

Diversification should not be pursued at the expense of fundamentals. It has to be done sensibly, with shares purchased only after research and thorough analysis show they fulfil your investment criteria. The smart investor can invest in a diversified portfolio of carefully selected individual high-quality shares with low correlation to one another. Diversification benefits are achieved by selecting high-quality shares from different sectors and of different market capitalisation – a mixture of large, medium-sized and small companies. A thoughtfully selected diversified portfolio should generate high returns with low risk.

Strategic asset allocation strategy

The core–satellite portfolio

The core–satellite investment strategy is a useful concept in designing a portfolio. The core or foundation of the portfolio may be a low-cost index fund, investment trust or ETF. The aim of the core fund is to replicate the market returns (known as beta). An ETF tracking the FTSE 100 index or the S&P 500 could be the core fund. Other candidates include a low-cost index tracker or a broad-based international investment trust with a history of progressive dividend growth. Alternatively, the core may be a selection of large blue chip UK companies. Around the core fund, the investor builds a satellite of individual shares or funds aiming to produce extra returns to the market (known as alpha).

All-ETF portfolio

ETFs have the qualities that perhaps make them the ideal collective investment vehicles for most investors: they have the lowest average total expense ratio (TER) of collective funds, they track different asset classes and sectors and can be bought and sold like individual shares. In the UK they can be bought without paying stamp duty. An investor can avoid the company-specific risks inherent in individual shares and instead develop a core–satellite strategy from an all-ETF portfolio.

A typical all-ETF portfolio may for instance have an ETF tracking the FTSE 100 as the core. The satellite is constructed from a diversified selection of specialist ETFs from sectors with low correlation to each other, for example utilities, commodities, real estate, energy, telecommunications, healthcare, transport and bonds. Ideally, each ETF is added during a period when that sector is out of favour and selling at a discount, though the long-term investor can also use a regular monthly savings plan and employ the benefits of pound-cost averaging.

Multi-manager and multi-asset fund of funds

New investors are often advised to consider multi-manager or multi-asset funds run by managers who aim to pool together the best-performing funds from various sectors like commodities, property, investment trusts and hedge funds and create a fund of funds. The manager therefore has responsibility for strategic asset allocation and diversity which may suit the novice amateur investor overwhelmed by the sheer number of available funds. Unfortunately, most of these multi-manager funds have prohibitively high costs. They suffer from a double whammy of fees – a management fee and the annual charges of the individual funds – leading to an average TER of about 2.21%. Since only a very small minority of managers have a consistent record of skilful asset allocation, the smart investor should avoid these expensive funds, opting instead for low-cost ETFs, investment trusts and index or tracker funds.

Tactical asset allocation strategy

Rebalancing

Tactical asset allocation dictates reducing the proportion of an outperforming asset to rebalance its relative value in the portfolio. This is based on the theory of reversion to mean

(RTM) where a period of outperformance by an asset is followed by relative underperformance as values oscillate around a mean. The investor is therefore advised to sell some outperforming shares to maintain their relative balance. However, the long-term equity investor should not always sell a stock merely on the basis of outperformance. A share price that has doubled in value could double again. The investor that sells a share that has doubled in price is attempting to time the market which, even for the most experienced investors, is a very difficult task. Investors may carry out a rebalancing exercise annually but TAA may lead to too frequent trading and excessive active portfolio management. The costs of frequent buying and selling can severely affect your returns and also deprive the investor of the long-term benefits of compounding reinvested dividends.

Rotation of monthly investment plan

A low-cost regular monthly investment plan can be used to develop a diversified portfolio and for a rotational tactical asset allocation strategy. This may be an all-ETF core–satellite portfolio. Instead of selling the well-performing share or fund in the portfolio, an alternative TAA strategy is to instead allocate the monthly investment to the share or ETF in the portfolio that is currently out of favour and selling at a reasonable valuation. A sector or stock may temporarily underperform due to a broker downgrade or market factors; for example, defensive sectors like pharmaceuticals and utilities may underperform during a cyclical recovery as investors chase riskier stocks. Underperformance may also occur because of industry-specific factors such as when tobacco company shares were under the cloud of litigation. Often short-term market sentiment against a sector or company may temporarily dent the share price. The smart investor therefore exploits these anomalies and rotates his monthly investment to the undervalued stock or fund in a diversified portfolio using a contrarian approach. Instead of selling your best performers, you allocate your monthly investment to the cheapest stock or ETF in the portfolio. This in the long term will reduce the average purchase price and the investor avoids putting funds into an overvalued stock.

CHAPTER 13

Lessons from a private investor

Lessons learned from over 30 years of investing:

- Shares confer part-ownership of a business.

- Learn how to read and understand company financial accounts and simple key ratios.

- Over the long run stocks and shares outperform other financial assets for the patient investor.

- Define your financial goals and objectives.

- Spend time researching your investments.

- Use broker recommendations sensibly.

- Use your everyday experiences and knowledge of an industry to your advantage.

- Start investing early.

- Know your temperament and psychological make-up, avoiding excessive greed and fear.

- Do not speculate but invest.

- Avoid excessive and erratic trading.

- Buy and hold quality companies in simple businesses you understand, with consistent growth in earnings and dividends, that are financially strong and profitable, with excellent long-term prospects and selling at reasonable valuations.

- Develop an investment thesis for every stock you buy.

- Avoid the herd instinct.

- Diversify sensibly.

- Be a proud shareholder – use the products and services.

- Invest in companies with high profit margins, high dividend cover, low debt to equity ratios and high return on capital employed relative to their competitors.

- Avoid companies trading on excessively high P/E ratios in relation to their historical mean.

- Stocks selling at a P/E ratio less than their growth rates (PEG of less than 1) are attractive.

- Invest regularly, employing pound-cost averaging.

- Do not try to time the market.

- Understand the power of compound interest.

- Reinvest all dividends.

- Be obsessive about keeping costs low.

- Employ low-cost share dealing execution-only nominee accounts using regular investment savings plans.

- If investing in funds select from simple low-cost tracker (index) funds, investment trusts and exchange traded funds (ETFs).

- Sell if the business fundamentals deteriorate.

- Be conscious of economic, global, regional and technological trends.

- Allocate assets according to your investment objectives and risk profile.